1367/78/2087   5ω~

399
RXS   Ntx(o)

THE ISLANDS SERIES

RHODES

THE ISLANDS SERIES

* Published in the United States by Stackpole
† Published in the United States by David & Charles Inc
The series is distributed in Australia by Wren Publishing Pty Ltd, Melbourne

RHODES

by *BRIAN DICKS*

DAVID & CHARLES : NEWTON ABBOT

STACKPOLE BOOKS : HARRISBURG

This edition first published in 1974
in Great Britain by
David & Charles (Holdings) Limited Newton Abbot Devon
in the United States in 1974 by
Stackpole Books Harrisburg Pa

ISBN 0 7153 6571 1 (*Great Britain*)
ISBN 0 8117 1435 7 (*United States*)

*Set in eleven on thirteen point Baskerville
and printed in Great Britain
by Latimer Trend & Company Ltd*

For

Michael Johnstone

CONTENTS

ILLUSTRATIONS

ILLUSTRATIONS

Unless otherwise acknowledged the photographs are from the author's collection.

IN TEXT

1 AN ISLAND IN CONTEXT

The Sporades are lean wolves and hunt in packs; waterless, eroded by the sun. They branch off on every side as you coast along the shores of Anatolia. Then towards afternoon the shaggy green of Kos comes up; and then, slithering out of the wintry blue the moist green flanks of Rhodes.

Lawrence Durrell

THE Aegean Sea is the heart of the Greek world and scattered within it are more than 1,900 islands and islets. Each is a world of its own, with its own customs, colours and shapes, and its own separate history. The Greeks speak of the islands as God's castaway stones, for when He had finished making the world the pieces left over were thrown into the Aegean Sea. Rhodes, by Aegean standards, is one of the big stones, but its distinction is not so much its larger body as its different face.

If possible the visitor to Rhodes for the first time should approach the island from the sea. From the deck of a ship, as the island looms in the distance, it is not difficult to conjure up the romantic images of its past. Here once stood a wonder of the ancient world, a colossus of the sun god Helios whose lofty proportions guided shipping to what was one of the richest and most powerful trading cities in antiquity. That Helios straddled the entrance to the Commercial Harbour is now considered a medieval confection, but it is a romantic view difficult to dislodge. Poetic fancy also enshrines the Middle Ages, for on Rhodes was the great Crusader fortress of the Knights of St John. Described as 'the most remarkable body of religious warriors the world has ever seen', images of banners and blazoned shields come to mind as the Knights defended the last bastion of Christianity in the eastern Mediterranean.

The colossus has gone and little remains of the city of antiquity, but the shadow of the Knights still falls across the island. As the ship enters the Commercial Harbour romanticism ends, for this is part of the medieval fortifications, and Rhodes is no fanciful Camelot. This solid citadel with its gates, towers and battlements was designed for defence and war and only by treachery could the enemy enter. Such an enemy was the Ottoman conqueror, Sultan Suleiman the Magnificent, and the minarets and domed mosques that punctuate the skyline above the battlements symbolise betrayal to the Turks by one of the Knights' own numbers.

The Gothic and oriental skyline, however, is but a backdrop to the activities of the port and it quickly becomes apparent that Rhodes has succeeded in domesticating the alien cultures of its past. Fishermen mending nets, small boys diving for coins, priests buying watermelons, mothers searching for children, vendors selling souvenirs, old men manipulating worry-beads, cab-drivers seeking fares—these and other scenes, accompanied by noise, frenzy and excitement, announce that this is the port of a typical Greek island.

An island is, by definition, a geographical entity and, as such, little justification is needed for studying it in depth or in isolation. Rhodes is most certainly 'a piece of land surrounded by water' but any discussion of its historical development and contemporary character would suffer if it was not stressed from the outset that the island is an integral part of the Aegean island community (Fig 1). Many have argued that Rhodes is the epitome of Greece, presenting in miniature an excellent illustration of the developments in human geography which correspond to the vicissitudes of history.

Fig 1   Greece and the Aegean

The islands of the Aegean Sea are divided geographically into distinct groups, according to their structure, configuration, and relation to continental foreshores. Rhodes is the most important member of the Dodecanese group which lies physically marginal to the south-western coast of Asia Minor between latitudes 35° 20′ and 37° 30′ N and longitudes 26° 15′ and 28° 40′ E. Together with the island of Crete, this archipelago constitutes the southernmost part of Greece.

The term 'Dodecanese' (*dodeka nisos*), meaning 'twelve islands' is a misnomer and only by a series of historical accidents has the group acquired its contemporary name. The essential

15

islands number *fourteen* in all and from north to south they are Patmos, Lipsos, Leros, Kalymnos, Kos, Astypalaea, Nisyros, Simi, Tilos, Chalki, Rhodes, Karpathos, Kasos and Kastello-rizzo (Fig 2), the latter lying 120km to the east of Rhodes. In addition there are at least forty islets, many of which are but uninhabited rocks and reefs. The combined surface area is

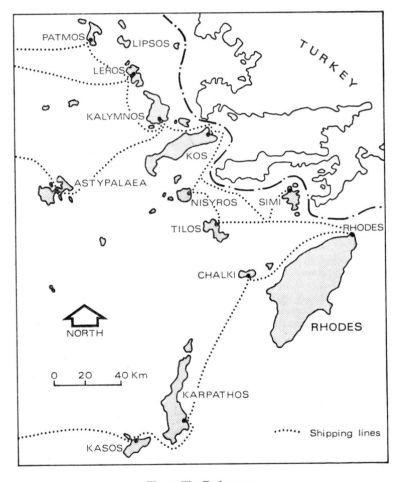

Fig 2 The Dodecanese

Page 17 (above) Aerial view of Rhodes city showing the harbours, the modern commercial quarter to the right, and the walled town in the background; (below) the port of St Paul at Lindos, one of the few natural harbours along the island's east coast

Page 18 (*above*) A modern cruise ship dwarfs the medieval walls of Rhodes' Commercial Harbour; (*below*) the active Mandraki Harbour with the Italian-built market and the Palace of the Grand Masters in the background

2,721sq km of which Rhodes comprises roughly one half (1,404sq km).

The archipelago is also known as the 'Sporades' (scattered), a name that still appears on many modern maps. Sporades is prefixed by 'Southern' to distinguish the group from the Northern Sporades in the central Aegean basin which include the islands of Skyros, Skopelos and Skiathos. 'Scattered' is perhaps a more useful and meaningful term, especially when the irregular arrangement of the group is compared with the more compact and contiguous distribution of the Cyclades islands.

Volonakis and other authors have traced the origin of the term 'Dodecanese' and it is interesting to note that when used by Byzantine historians of the eighth and ninth centuries it referred to the Cyclades which formed a distinct civil and ecclesiastic province. In the tenth century the Aegean islands were administratively subdivided between Cyclades and Sporades and the term 'Dodecanese' fell into disuse. It reappears when the Emperor Baldwin II of Constantinople gave 'Dodecanese' to his son-in-law and the context shows that the Cycladic Duchy of Naxos was meant. Heirs to the duchy became known as Dukes of the Dodecanese.

With the Turkish occupation of the Aegean, 'Dodecanese' came to be popularly applied to those islands off the Asia Minor coast, from Samos to Rhodes, which had been given special administrative and commercial privileges by the Ottoman conqueror Suleiman the Magnificent. Imperial firmans by succeeding sultans confirmed and extended these liberties which in sum formed a charter of local autonomy. Neither Rhodes nor Kos, however, were fortunate in obtaining these favours and, when in 1908 they were withdrawn, 'Dodecanese' became the collective title for those islands which resisted Turkish encroachment on their historic rights.

Between 1912 and 1945 when the Italians administered the archipelago a variety of names became fashionable. These included Tredeci Isole (Thirteen Islands), the Sporades, and Rhodes and the Sporades. Finally the official title became Rhodes and the Dodecanese, of which the former is the administrative capital and, commercially, the most important island of the group.

Whatever the changing political title of these islands, few regions in the world have had such a turbulent history as the Dodecanese. The reason is geographical, particularly the location aspect, for they lie nearer to Asia Minor than to mainland Greece. Rhodes has often been compared to a great ship anchored off the coast of Turkey, for whereas it is 451km from Athens and Piraeus, the Asia Minor coast is only 18km across the Sea of Marmaris. Rhodes also lies on sea routes that join three continents and is 402km from Izmir, 442 from Limassol, 576 from Alexandria, 628 from Beirut and 724 from Istanbul.

The island reveals vividly the conditioning influence of this geographical position, one in which insularity proved the very antithesis of isolation. Throughout antiquity, and at various periods during historical times, Rhodes was the battleground of contending cultures and religions and of conflicting political and commercial interests. The strategic importance of the island was the cause of successive invasions and constantly it lay at the mercy of the dominant sea powers of the eastern Mediterranean. Greece, Rome, Byzantium, the Knights of St John of Jerusalem, Turks and Italians make up the greater part of the fabric of the past, though Venetian and Genoese influence was also considerable.

Rhodes lay along a profound cultural divide in the Mediterranean, one that separated the basin into Moslem and Christian halves. Throughout the Middle Ages the island was the political pawn in the ideological game between Western Europe and the Moslem East and its situation, together with its naval bases, made it a valuable screen when held by either eastern or western powers. The city of Rhodes, together with Famagusta in Cyprus, were considered to be the two major strategic holds of the West against the Turk. During World War II Rhodes was regarded as a major key to both British and German strategy in the Aegean. Following the fall of Italy the island was occupied by German forces until its recapture and liberation by the British and Greeks. In 1948, Rhodes and the Dodecanese were officially recognised as part of the Kingdom of Greece and reconstruction of its economy commenced. Like Crete, Rhodes had an advantage over mainland Greece in avoiding civil war.

To Rhodes, therefore, insularity has been a feeble defender against outside domination and the succession of occupying forces has inevitably left its mark on the island, not only in a physical sense, but also on its contemporary population. In such circumstances, the emergence of, at one extreme, a highly nationalistic population or, at the other extreme, a cosmopolitan community devoid of a distinctive overall identity, would have seemed equally probable. Neither of these, however, approaches an adequate description of the contemporary Rhodian population. The Rhodians' awareness of, and pride in, their Greekness has, throughout history, associated the island with the Greek world in general. National patriotism has always taken precedence over local parochialism. It was this strong assertion of the Hellenic nature of the island's culture, enriched rather than created by forces from outside, that was sufficient to sustain Rhodes during its long periods of occupation and oppression. Today, the island is reaching new levels of development and prosperity. Much of this is related to the increasing numbers of tourists to the island and the economic future of Rhodes may well lie in the commercialisation of its rich and varied past.

2   THE RHODIAN ENVIRONMENT

IN antiquity the island now known as Rhodes went under a
variety of descriptive names. The general shape and configuration of the island were embodied in the names *Stadia*
(due to its ellipsoidal or almond shape), *Trinakria* (an island
with three principal headlands—though, unfortunately, there
are four), and *Korymbia* (from its resemblance to a laurel leaf).
Other names included *Attavyris* (from the highest mountain),
Olyessa (possibly due to its many earthquakes), *Poeissa* (which
referred to its richness and abundant vegetation), *Makaria*
(meaning paradise, and justified by the island's natural beauty),
Asteria (from its clear atmosphere) and *Ophiousa* (from the
poisonous snakes that according to tradition inflicted many
deaths on the local inhabitants). These names were passing
fancies, but each reflects, or emphasises, some significant aspect
of the island's physical environment.

STRUCTURE AND TOPOGRAPHY

The physical geography of Rhodes illustrates most clearly the
island's close association with both mainland Greece and the
Asia Minor landmass. Rhodes, together with the other Aegean
islands, continues the geological structure and configuration
of Greece into western Turkey, emphasising the common
parentage of the whole Aegean region. From the central
mountainous core of Arcadia in the Peloponnesus a main
highland chain can be traced southwards to the island of
Kythera and then through Crete, Karpathos and Rhodes into

Asia Minor. These islands, which form the 'Cretan arc', mark the southern structural limit of the Aegean basin and separate it from the main basin of the eastern Mediterranean. They owe their origin to tectonic upheavals and structural disturbances in Tertiary times and are, in fact, the exposed summits of mountain chains now submerged in the Aegean basin. The intricate pattern of the Aegean coast and its islands, however, is the result of a complex geological history and adjustments to the highly fractured strata of the area, along structural lines of weakness, still take place.

Rhodian legends and the writings of early geographers such as Strabo and Pliny, explain the formation of the island in terms of geological catastrophes producing periods of submergence and emergence. Diodorus also reports some traditions about a great flood in Rhodes in which there was a heavy loss of life when the low-lying parts of the island became inundated. Recent geological research, together with archaeological investigation, has added much weight to the argument of oscillations in sea level. The presence of marine fossil shells at the foot of hills and even on mountain tops indicates the magnitude of land and sea movements, as do the raised terraces of the east coast, deeply dissected by stream courses, and the tabular form of the island's hills. Such movements, however, have not been uniform in one direction, but have registered both positive and negative changes of land in relation to sea level, the result being a landscape with a most complicated geological and erosional history.

Geological instability is also evident in other forms. Rhodes, like the adjacent areas of Greece and Turkey, belongs to one of the world's main regions most severely affected by earth tremors. The Aegean and the Mediterranean are of geologically recent origin and their fractured edges along the Turkish coastlands constitute zones of major weakness. In particular, the sea troughs that penetrate into Turkey are subject to the frequent movement of strata along their faulted edges. Rhodes averages about two severe earthquakes a century with minor tremors every year. The famous Hellenistic colossus was destroyed by an earthquake in 227 BC and the ramparts and towers of the medieval Knights of St John were repeatedly destroyed or weakened. An ancient stele, discovered at Cameiros, bears the dateless inscription 'to the memory of the victims of the earthquake', and similar monuments are common on the island, particularly around Rhodes town. Within the old town itself, and in Lindos, arched buttresses across streets emphasise the need for protection against earth tremors. There are records of major earthquakes in the years 157, 227, 515, 1304, 1364, 1481, 1851 and 1863, and during this century, Lindos in particular, especially the southern part of the settlement, has suffered much from earthquakes. The only volcano at present active in Greece is that of the Cycladic island Thera, better known by its Italian name Santorini. To the north-west of Rhodes, however, 60km away, is the almost circular island of Nisyros which is of volcanic origin. It is probable that in pre-history volcanic eruptions and seismic activity, accompanied by tidal waves, were responsible for the flooding which traditionally affected Rhodes and other Aegean islands. Such a theory has been further developed by Marinatos and Schaeffer with particular reference to the destruction of the Minoan Empire of Crete by natural causes.

On Rhodes, the geological strike of the Cretan arc assumes a south-west to north-east direction, producing an island 84km long and narrowing to points at the northern and southern ends in Capes Kumburnu and Prassonissi. Its maximum width is 38km between Cape Lardos in the east and Cape Armenistas in the west. Basically the island consists of a core of resistant rocks, chiefly Cretaceous limestone, overlain by more recent and softer rocks of Tertiary age (Fig 3). In its centre, however, formations of pre-Cretaceous age are exposed in the core of the major folded structures and these, together with the limestones, are principally responsible for the major relief features of the island.

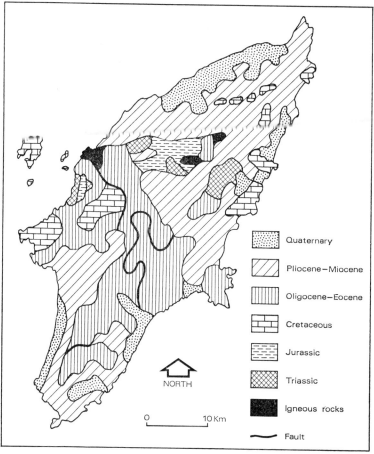

Fig 3   Rhodes, solid geology

Repeated earth movements of a local character have complicated the folded structure and subsequent erosion of the softer beds, followed by marine and lacustrine deposits in areas of subsidence, make the details of geological history difficult to interpret.

Much of the south is composed of Oligocene and Eocene deposits which vary greatly in composition and character both

25

areally and from horizon to horizon. Sandstones, limestones, silts and conglomerates are common and at the base of the Eocene beds is a thick deposit of flysch. In the north, Pliocene and Miocene beds predominate but they are also found in the south. They give rise to outcrops of sandstone, marl, limestone and conglomerate. The Quaternary deposits are mainly beds of marine clays and river alluvium occupying coastal locations, chiefly in the north and the extreme south of the island. From the economic point of view the island is lacking in minerals but to the student of pure geology and to the fossil collector, Rhodes offers a rich field for investigation.

With the exception of a number of imposing summits the nature of the topography of Rhodes is highly dissected rather than truly mountainous and takes its character from the softer rocks of Tertiary age. These, though variable in quality and resistance, are intersected by steep-sided ravines, indicative of the extent of recent elevation and active erosion. A confused sort of topography is characteristic, of hills, and basins hollowed out in softer terrain. The highest altitudes (Fig 4) are reached in the west in a series of summits which mark the main watershed and subdivide the island into a number of hilly masses. In the north, and almost midway between the eastern and western coasts, is an area which reaches altitudes of between 430 and 500m. It has important passes at Psinthos and Koscinisti. Southwards it is bounded by the Profita range which trends in an east–west direction with summits in Speriali (507m) and Elia (773m). The range is prolonged eastward to Mount Archangelos (512m) and westward into a chain of rocky islands that lie between Cape Kopria and the island of Chalki. The western coast is dominated by Mount Attavyros (1,356m) and from it a south-west trending spur, Acromytis (592m), reaches the sea in Cape Monolithos. A long eastward ridge from Attavyros ends in the Lardos promontory beyond Mounts Kalathos (400m) and Marmari (466m). The Skiathi area in the south reaches an altitude of 358m and is connected to the

Attavyros system by the Strongili ridge (540m). The Skiathi uplands sink almost to sea level in the Kattavia lowlands, beyond which a north-west to south-east ridge connects Capes Karavola and Prassonissi.

The upland areas furnish abundant winter rainfall and give rise to a considerable number of streams, although few are

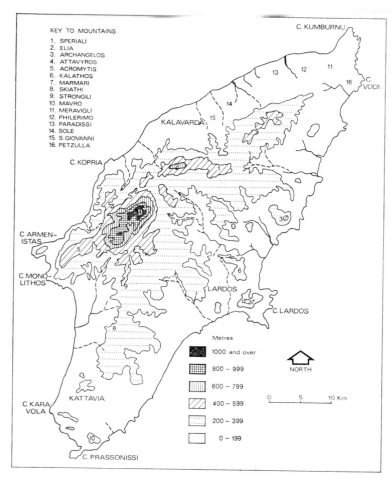

KEY TO MOUNTAINS
1. SPERIALI
2. ELIA
3. ARCHANGELOS
4. ATTAVYROS
5. ACROMYTIS
6. KALATHOS
7. MARMARI
8. SKIATHI
9. STRONGILI
10. MAVRO
11. MERAVIGLI
12. PHILERIMO
13. PARADISSI
14. SOLE
15. S.GIOVANNI
16. PETZULLA

C. KUMBURNU
C. VODI
C. KOPRIA
KALAVARDA
C. ARMEN-ISTAS
C. MONO-LITHOS
LARDOS
C. LARDOS
KATTAVIA
C. KARA-VOLA
C. PRASSONISSI

Metres
1000 and over
800 – 999
600 – 799
400 – 599
200 – 399
0 – 199

NORTH

0   5   10 Km

Fig 4   Rhodes, relief and configuration

27

perennial. In spite of the fact, however, that rainfall is mostly from the north-west, the principal drainage runs eastwards (Fig 5) and streams cut back deeply into the watershed ranges. Much of the eroded material has been carried seawards to form coastal plains and beaches, but as some parts of the coast have sunk, and others risen, there are examples of both dry raised beaches and alluvial coastal plains with choked river outlets.

The discontinuous and somewhat restricted coastal areas have always held a greater attraction for settlement than the dissected hill country of the interior. The most extensive lowland is in the north-west, extending from Rhodes town to Kalavarda. It is bounded by a low cliff seawards through which streams have cut deep gullies, and sections of it are silted and swampy. This lowland is commanded by a series of table-topped outliers which are erosional remnants of interior hills. Meravigli, Philerimo and Paradissi are examples, and further to the south-west it is interrupted by a series of upland spurs such as Sole and San Giovanni.

In the north-east the watershed plateau slopes gently eastwards to form a coastal area which is closed abruptly in the north by the Petzulla ridge, ending in Cape Vodi. Southwards to Archangelos it becomes more extensive and from Malona to Vlicha the silt from the rivers Platanero, Makkaris and Gadouras has produced a littoral lowland up to two miles in width. The lower reaches of these rivers are wide and marshy and the lowland is bounded southwards by the precipitous Kalathos ridge. Beyond Cape Lardos a series of disconnected coastal tracts occur, based on the regular alignment of streams which drain north-west to south-east. In the south-west, from Cape Karavola to Cape Monolithos the area is low and open with sandy beaches. Its main stream, Kourkoutachi, rises above Siana and has a wide upper basin with a silted lower course. Southwards it merges into the Kattavia lowlands much of which is swampy and liable to sea-flooding in stormy weather.

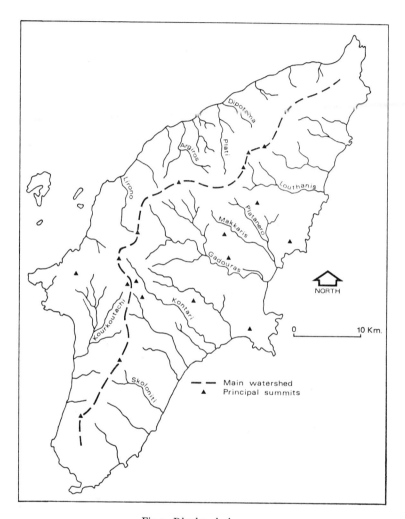

Fig 5 Rhodes, drainage

RHODES

CLIMATE

In general terms Rhodes experiences a Mediterranean climate in which seasonal rhythm of temperature, rainfall and weather is strongly marked. The main characteristics are hot, dry summers, mild winters, clear skies with abundant sunshine, and rainfall that is highly concentrated, mostly in the form of heavy showers during winter. This generalised pattern, however, is subject to a number of influences which produce local peculiarities. Rhodes lies on the margin of two distinct Mediterranean weather regions—the Aegean Sea and the eastern Mediterranean. It therefore shares some of the characteristics of both, but furthermore it is affected by its proximity to the continental highlands of south-west Anatolia. Within the island the chief factor modifying climate is altitude, and the detailed character of relief and aspect introduces further localised nuances.

Characteristic of both the Aegean and the eastern Mediterranean basin are the 'Etesian' (Turkish 'Meltemi') north and north-west winds which blow from the high pressure area of eastern Europe during summer. Lying close to Asia Minor, Rhodes has a modified north wind, but summer is still characterised by great atmospheric stability and uniformity and cloudless skies. On average, Rhodes experiences 130–50 cloudless days, mostly in summer, when cyclonic disturbances are almost unknown and rain practically absent. The pronounced summer period lasts through June to September and weather changes little from day to day. The only variation is the daily 'imbat' alternation of land and sea breezes which becomes regular in May and June and lasts until autumn.

The breezes are related to the unequal diurnal heating of land and sea and to the resulting development of local pressure differences. During the day the land heats rapidly and pressure falls, initiating a sea breeze. It rises about 9.30 am, but by late afternoon the pressure difference between land and sea is small and a period of calm follows. After sunset the land loses heat more rapidly than the sea and a land breeze blows until early morning. A period of calm again follows until the sea breeze rises. Since few parts of Rhodes are more than ten miles from the coast, the greater part of the island experiences these diurnal changes. The major control is altitude and the local breezes cease at about 500–650m where they merge with the prevalent wind system. The breezes are of considerable practical importance since they prevent excessively high summer temperatures, despite the bright unclouded sky. In the past, local fishing was governed largely by the daily rhythm of these breezes.

Towards the end of September the monotonous rhythm of the Rhodian summer is disturbed by a break in the regularity of the north winds and by the approach of depressions moving west to east through the Mediterranean basin. Autumn introduces a fall in temperature, but the waters of the Mediterranean remain at a high temperature and the weather is warm and damp—at times unpleasantly so. The cyclonic storms of the winter season often arrive suddenly and rain is usually heavy. A fall of 4in in a day is not uncommon. Compared with the temperate climates of Western Europe, however, the number of rain-days is low and winter is interspersed with days of brilliant sunshine. Rhodian figures record an average of 136hr of sunshine in January (which is one of the wettest months), and between 65 and 85 rain-days a year. The annual rainfall total rarely exceeds 35in, although it should be pointed out that this total is considerably higher than that experienced in most parts of southern Greece.

The winter storms continue until April or May, but with diminishing force and with lengthening intervals between them. There is usually a period of calm in April and intermittent spells of the summer north wind bringing cool bright days with cold nights. After early May rain is almost unknown until October.

The following table summarises the main seasonal aspects of

Rhodian climate (rainfall totals in inches and temperatures in degrees Fahrenheit):

	Number of rain-days	Mean rainfall	Average max temperature	Average min temperature	Mean temperature
January	14	5·4	63	25	49
February	12	5·5	65	34	51
March	10	4·6	71	34	52
April	8	1·1	82	39	59
May	3	1·0	87	54	68
June	3	0·2	90	59	74
July	0·5	0·1	92	66	79
August	0·5	0·1	93	65	78
September	1	0·1	95	52	72
October	5	1·9	86	49	67
November	8	5·4	76	39	59
December	12	7·7	67	29	52
Total	77·0	33·1			

Mean temperatures for the summer months vary between 74° F and 79° F, although maximum temperatures of 90–95° F are common. Altitude lowers temperatures but even in the foothills of Mount Attavyros the monthly means for July and August remain around 73° F. January and February are the coldest months, but frost is rare and snow falls only in exceptionally hard winters.

FLORA AND FAUNA

The composition and character of Rhodian vegetation has probably not altered much since prehistoric times, with two major exceptions: the first, the diminution of forest timber, especially the cypress; and the second, the introduction of numerous fruit trees and other cultivated crops. In antiquity the island was noted for its richness and luxuriant vegetation and even today its flora, particularly its wealth of flowering plants, is exceptional. Rhodes stands in marked contrast to many Aegean islands, especially those in the Cyclades group, and a number in the Dodecanese, where soil erosion and the degeneration of natural vegetation cover has produced a stark, rocky landscape. The composition of Rhodian flora illustrates clearly the island's geographical position and its physical connection with neighbouring landmasses in earlier times. Out of a total of around 700 recorded species, of which 557 are widespread throughout the Mediterranean, 88 are indigenous to the eastern basin, 58 are shared with Turkey and Syria, 11 with Turkey and Crete and 20 species and varieties are peculiar to Rhodes itself.

Both the natural vegetation and the cultivated crops are closely related to the climate of the island. The absence of summer rains limits vegetation to xerophytic (drought-resisting) plants, though adaptation to such conditions varies from species to species. Some have leaves which minimise evaporation, others have a thick bark, while some, like the wild olive and vine, have long tap-roots which find water at lower levels. Such highly adapted plants also include hardy species of grasses which are quick to take advantage of spring rains. They resist the summer drought by requiring a short growing season. Other grasses survive because of their extensive root system and tough, wiry, foliage.

Rhodes is lofty enough in heights such as Attavyros, Elia and Acromytis to show an altitudinal gradation of vegetation, although this is now much modified as the result of centuries of human settlement. From sea level to around 400m the island is either cultivated or under rough pasture. Above this limit to about 700m there is some cultivation but mixed scrub communities (including *phrygana*) and deciduous shrubs are common. From 700m deciduous and coniferous forest trees predominate, but there are no areas of the island high enough to feature oak scrub, dwarf shrubs and highland pasture.

In antiquity there are references to Rhodes being covered by

33

thick forests of pine and cypress, but for at least 3,000 years the character and extent of this woodland has been under attack. Deforestation has been reckless and during the Turkish period alone trees were felled without thought for the future and timber was in constant demand for the shipyards of Constantinople and Smyrna. Deforestation was accelerated by the cutting of leafy branches for winter fodder and the depredations of grazing livestock, particularly goats, has led to widespread destruction. The principal forest trees are pines (*P. brutia* and *halepensis*), cypresses (*C. sempervirens* and *horizontalis*), oaks (*Quercus aigelops, coccifera, infectoria, robur* and *lanuginosa*) and junipers (*J. macrocarpa* and *phoenicia*). The plane (*Platanus orientalis*) grows wild and is cultivated where moisture is sufficient. Wild species of pear, carob, medlar and turpentine are common, together with areas occupied by wild olive, vine and fig.

Centuries of interference with the island's vegetation cover has led to a secondary growth of degraded vegetation types, collectively known as maquis. These scrubby plant communities are common to all long-settled lands sharing a Mediterranean climate. In appearance the maquis is infinitely varied. In places it takes the form of a stunted woodland dotted with conifers and oaks or it can become a tangled, almost impenetrable thicket. It may also be continuous or patchy in appearance, but everywhere woody evergreen bushes are the chief elements. In time the maquis may return to woodland, but the impoverishment of the soil, consequent on deforestation, and the almost certain continued interference of grazing animals and man, generally prevents this.

About one-fifth of the total area of Rhodes ranks as high maquis and attempts are being made to conserve it as forest. Another fifth is low maquis, which is scrub and waste and can be used only as poor-grade pasture. The composition of both the high and low maquis communities varies considerably with conditions of aspect, slope, rock type and soil cover, but all species are again characterised by their adaptation to dry con-

Page 35 (*above*) The congested old town of Rhodes seen from the medieval battlements;
(*below*) the northern hotel and tourist section of modern Rhodes

Page 36 (left) A street in the old town of Rhodes. The linking arches provide protection against earthquakes; (below) the famous mole of the windmills and the French tower, Mandraki Harbour

ditions. Myrtle, genista, lentisk, cistus, lavender, thyme, and other aromatic plants are major constituents of the scrub communities and along water courses the oleander flourishes. Another characteristic of the maquis vegetation is the rich spring flowering season for plants which lie dormant during the summer heat and germinate with the first winter rains.

Deforestation has been the chief cause of a great reduction in the numbers and varieties of Rhodes' wild life. Snakes are still common on the island and one small species is poisonous. The larger varieties are harmless. Other reptiles include the water tortoise and the lizard—the largest, the 'Rhodes dragon' (*Agama stellio*), grows to 14in. It is, however, the deer which is particularly associated with the island and it is said to have been introduced in the Middle Ages by the Knights of St John. Unfortunately, the restrictions on hunting enforced by the Knights were ignored during the Turkish period and it was necessary for the Italians to reintroduce the deer in the early decades of this century. They can be seen on the forested slopes of the Profita range and in captivity in special enclosures surrounding the medieval walls of Rhodes town. Other fauna include the fox, hare, badger, marten and hedgehog, and common birds are the partridge, jackdaw and jay.

The island's productive animals are common to all Europe, but those better adapted to rocky, semi-arid hill country, such as the goat, sheep, ass and mule, are more prevalent than the pig, horse and cow. Camels, though common on the Asiatic mainland, are only occasionally used on Rhodes.

SOILS AND HYDROGRAPHY

Whereas foreign influence in Rhodes used the island for its commercial and strategic advantages, the native population has always been tied to the island's agricultural potential and hence to its soil and water resources. Mediterranean soils as a whole have not received the same detailed attention as those of

C

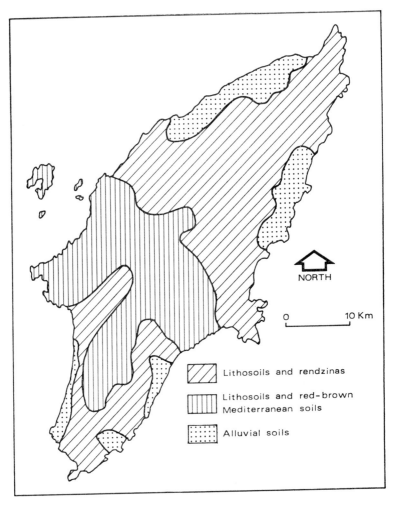

NORTH

0   10 Km

Lithosoils and rendzinas

Lithosoils and red-brown
Mediterranean soils

Alluvial soils

Fig 6   Rhodes, major soil groups

temperate regions and the soil groups depicted on Fig 6 must be regarded as broad generalisations only, and tentative, until a detailed investigation is undertaken. Rhodian soils bear a close relationship with the island's geology and parent material but equally significant factors in their formation and fertility are climate, particularly the vital relationship between precipitation and evaporation, the interference of man and animals and the nuances of relief, especially slope and aspect.

Soils derived from calcareous parent materials are among the commonest on the island and the broad division is between red-brown 'Mediterranean' soils and rendzinas. The former are related to the Oligocene-Eocene and older geological formations and the latter chiefly to the areas of Pliocene-Miocene deposits. The rendzinas form a thin layer of darkish loam with a base composed of rock fragments. They are often subject to erosion damage which is particularly serious due to their shallow depth. Throughout the island, also, are areas of lithosoils which are commonly found on steep slopes. Although termed 'soils' they show little soil development and form a very thin cover over bedrock and are agriculturally insignificant. In time they can develop into rendzinas. The areas of great agricultural potential are the coastal districts with alluvial soils. They have shallow water-tables and their moister surface tends to be rich in organic material.

The alluvial areas are the principal irrigated districts of the island, but elsewhere farming and settlement is dependent on the seasonal rainfall regime. Rhodes has no large rivers and very few perennial streams. Those that flow in summer are precarious, but the presence of oleanders and other shrubs along watercourses, apparently dry, indicate that water is present some feet below the surface. In winter the streams are often turbulent and many have steep torrent beds which bring down debris to form wide boulder-strewn flood plains. The streams are liable to become choked and to change their courses, while most of the finer silt eroded from upland areas is lost in inshore waters.

Stream and soil erosion, therefore, is most active in winter, especially where slopes are steep and the vegetation cover degraded.

Fortunately for settlement, deep-seated springs occur throughout the island, usually where massive limestone or sandstone formations rest on impervious beds of clays or marls. Well water is also common in the stratified sands and shales, and all villages are supplied by either a well or natural spring. As an extra precaution, however, rain-cisterns are attached to houses to collect surplus rainfall for use during the summer drought.

3   THE ISLAND IN ANTIQUITY

RHODES resembles other Greek islands and many mainland localities in that its earliest beginnings are lost in
the mists of prehistory and mythology. The name
'Rhodes', itself, is of uncertain derivation and there has been
much speculation over its origin. An impressive, but not very
plausible theory, is that it derives from the Phoenician word
jarod or *erod*, meaning snake. Even allowing for the dropping of
the first syllable and the subsequent Hellenisation of the word,
most authorities are unconvinced by this explanation. A more
likely, but by no means certain, interpretation stems from
archaeological investigation. This has brought to light Rhodian
coins with the head of the sun god Helios on one side and the
blossom of a flower, possibly a rose or a pomegranate, on the
reverse side. One school of thought claims that the island's name
comes from *rodon*, the Greek word for rose, and another
supports *roiden*, the word for pomegranate. Whatever the bloom
may be, and it seems more likely that it was the indigenous
pomegranate, there is little doubt that it became the emblem
of the city of Rhodes after its foundation in the early fifth
century BC.

If the argument is still unconvincing, the final resort is
mythology itself and the legendary nymph, *Rhodon*. Custom
has named Rhodes Apollo's island though legend indicates that
in fact it was the domain of Helios. Confusion arose as the result
of the similarity of the two gods, and the merging of the myths
into one cycle clouding their separate identities. Apollo was a
sun god only—the god of sunlight—but Helios was the god

personifying the sun itself. Pindar relates the legend that when they were allotting islands, Zeus and the Olympian deities forgot to provide for Helios. Fortunately a virgin island rose from the sea to solve Zeus' dilemma and Rhodon, daughter of Poseidon, became the spouse of Helios. According to the tale Rhodon and Helios had seven sons, one of which, Kerkafos, fathered the three heroes Ialysos, Cameiros and Lindos who in turn founded the great Rhodian cities of antiquity which bore their names.

THE THREE ANCIENT CITIES

Very little is known of the early prehistoric cultures of the island and the mythological creation of Rhodes was obviously an attempt by the ancients to account for something that was inexplicable at the time without an adequate knowledge of geology. It is surprising how far the poetic fancy of the Greeks comes near to the truth. Even though today we cannot accept, literally, that Rhodes rose from the sea, it is fact that the island was the product of oscillations in sea level throughout post-glacial times. The legendary account of the three ancient cities probably arose out of a definite situation and was no doubt intended to achieve something, even if only, as has been suggested, to explain away the unpalatable fact that the cities were founded by Dorian invaders.

Though there are traces of Stone Age occupation in the Aspri Petra cave on Kos, it appears that the Dodecanese islands in general received the various Aegean cultures in their later stages of development. According to Thucydides, among the first groups to invade Rhodes were the piratical Carians from the Asia Minor mainland. They were followed by the Phoenicians whose movements are better documented. Arriving from the eastern Mediterranean they recognised the positional and commercial significance of Rhodes and used it as a base before moving westwards to Crete and beyond. There is evidence of

Phoenician occupation at Ialysos in the north-western part of the island.

Around 1500 BC several trading outposts were founded by Minoan immigrants from Crete, and Ialysos was again selected as a site. The progenitors of the Greeks and the Greek language, however, were the Achaeans who arrived in Rhodes roughly a century later. They came from Mycenaean cities in southern Greece and built fortified citadels on hilltops dominating fertile coastal plains. Their presence lived on in the name Ialysos Achaia whose hill was crowned with one of their strongholds. Rhodes, together with Kos, Kalymnos and other Dodecanese islands became flourishing Mycenaean centres and in Homeric times Rhodes is represented as aiding the Achaean attack on Troy.

The period of Mycenaean influence came to an end on Rhodes somewhere around the middle of the twelfth century BC. In their wake came the Greek-speaking Dorians whose colonisation of the island formed but a small part of an extensive period of migration and conquest that swept much of the Greek world. Knowledge of the period down to 800 BC is vague and incomplete, but it is evident that these years saw the genesis of a new chapter in civilisation. They mark the great transition of power from people whose only defence was weapons of bronze to people who wielded iron.

Mycenaean society, as noted by Homer, was one of tribal divisions ruled by kings or chieftains who held regular council under the presidency of a kind of feudal overlord. By 800 BC a completely new system appeared in which the individual was free to develop his political, intellectual and aesthetic capacity. This was to find expression in the rise of the *polis* or the city state, each with its own life and system of government, its own industry and commerce. There is no doubt as to the Dorian domination of the island: it is confirmed by Pindar and Thucydides, and Strabo wrote 'the Rhodians are Dorians and so are the inhabitants of Halicarnassus, Knidos and Kos'.

Homer mentions the three cities of Ialysos, Cameiros and Lindos, which under the aegis of the Dorians were to grow into rich and powerful independent states.

Knowledge of the form and function of these early Rhodian cities comes from nineteenth-century excavations, and, more particularly, from the extensive work undertaken by the Italians this century. The publication of their discoveries, *Clara Rhodos*, is a monumental work which runs to nine volumes. It appears that both Lindos and Ialysos followed closely the typical form of the early city states, utilising to the greatest degree the defensive possibilities of their sites to control areas of potentially rich agricultural land and harbours. Thus the settlements were divided into two sections, the acropolis or high city, which was the local stronghold, and the lower section which was devoted to manufacturing and trading activities. The acropolis of Ialysos occupied a broad east-west plateau on the summit of the 292m-high Mount Philerimos. From this natural fortress the city extended downslope towards the modern villages of Trianda and Kremasti. Ialysos was first excavated in the nineteenth century by Salzman and Biliotti and later by the Italian archaeologists Majuri and Jacobi in 1914 and 1929–32. The excavations, together with chance discoveries, have revealed an extensive necropolis with graves and vases dating from Mycenaean times. Other attractions of the site include a fourth-century Doric temple dedicated to Athena and Zeus Polieus and a similarly dated fountain revealed in 1926 following an earth-slip. Ialysos possessed no harbour and a considerable distance separated the civil settlement from its acropolis. Thus, it was exposed to enemy attacks and was an easy prey for pirates.

Lindos occupied a central position on the eastern coast of Rhodes. The town developed around a natural acropolis of high headland (116m) whose undulating summit (130m long by 127m wide) formed an ideal defensive stronghold. The flank of the headland, falling abruptly to the sea, made an impregnable fortress, with the only means of approach being from the north. Other advantages included good anchorage in the form of the small land-locked bay to the south (Port of St Paul) and a larger, but equally sheltered harbour to the north (Fig 7). Lindos became the largest maritime city of the island and by the sixth century BC its trading relations had extended to Egypt, Cyprus and Phoenicia. One theory for the Lindians' maritime

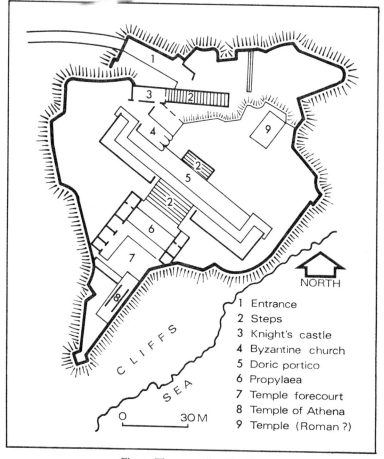

1 Entrance
2 Steps
3 Knight's castle
4 Byzantine church
5 Doric portico
6 Propylaea
7 Temple forecourt
8 Temple of Athena
9 Temple (Roman ?)

CLIFFS

SEA

NORTH

0   30 M

Fig 7   The acropolis of Lindos

strength has been related to the infertile, stony ground around the city which forced its inhabitants to turn to the sea as traders and fishermen. Their ambitions, however, reached far beyond coastal waters, for colonists from Lindos founded Parthenopea (the forerunner of Naples) and Gela in Sicily. They also explored and settled coastal areas in Provence and eastern Spain.

Lindos also developed as a major religious centre on Rhodes, focusing around the Temple of Athena on the acropolis. A Danish expedition under Kinch and Blinkenberg excavated Lindos between 1902 and 1914 and studies have continually taken place since, including that of another Dane, Einar Dyggve, in 1952. According to Dyggve the off-centre position of the temple was dictated by the presence directly beneath it, in the face of the cliff, of a sacred grotto. A temple on the site existed from at least the tenth century BC, but the contemporary ruins, faithful to the Doric order, date between 348 and 208 BC. One of the most interesting finds from Lindos is the Temple Chronicle, discovered in 1904 and now in Copenhagen. It records gifts to the goddess, allegedly donated by mythological and historical characters, and also records miraculous apparitions of the goddess in time of Rhodian peril.

The necessity for a local strong-point seems to have had less of an influence on the siting of Cameiros (Fig 8). The city occupied a natural bowl in the hillside, suspended above the coast, and it had neither acropolis nor fortifications. Excavations by Salzman and Biliotti in 1859 and by the Italians after 1929 brought to light an almost complete ground plan of the city, revealing streets and avenues, individual dwellings, temples and shrines. In the upper part of the city, which rises to 125m, are the ruins of public buildings, together with large cisterns that were part of an advanced water-supply system, using aqueducts, dating from the sixth century BC.

The years following the formation of the Rhodian city states marked what was essentially a period of experiment in methods of government. The three cities remained politically independent

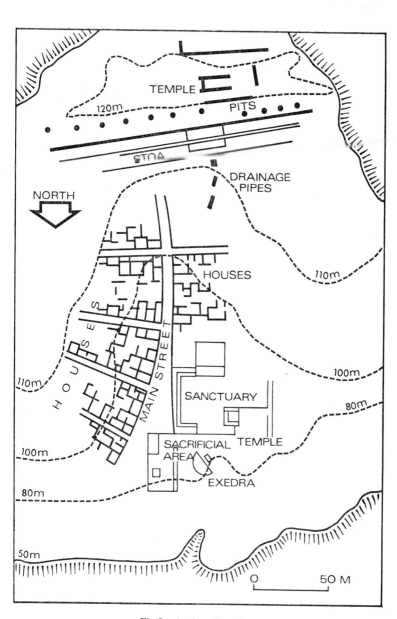

TEMPLE

120m

PITS

STOA

DRAINAGE
PIPES

NORTH

110m

HOUSES

H O U S E S

100m

MAIN STREET

SANCTUARY

80m

110m

100m

SACRIFICIAL
AREA

TEMPLE

80m

EXEDRA

50m

0   50 M

Fig 8   Ancient Cameiros

but since the island straddled the route of westward migrations and trading connections between Greece and Asia Minor, close relationships were established between the cities and neighbouring island and mainland communities. Ialysos, Lindos and Cameiros subsequently united with Kos and the Asiatic cities of Knidos and Halicarnassus to form the Dorian Hexapolis, a religious, economic and political confederation (Fig 9).

The league had its capital at the Temple of Apollo on the Triopian promontory at Knidos and also acted as a balance of power against the Ionian states which had amalgamated earlier and established their sanctuary at the Temple of Artemis at

Fig 9   The Dorian Hexapolis

Ephesus. The great danger to the early city states came from Persia with its warlike leaders such as Cyrus and Darius. The famous defeat of Persian forces by the Athenians at Marathon in 491 BC was only the opening skirmish in a series of Persian assaults on Greece and in 490 BC Rhodes felt the brunt of Persian attacks. By 478 BC the island had joined the Delian Confederacy as subject allies of Athens, but in 411 BC, towards the end of the Peloponnesian War, the Rhodians revolted against Athens in favour of Sparta.

THE FOUNDATION OF RHODES

During the classical (fifth and fourth centuries BC) and Hellenistic (late fourth century to 31 BC) periods Rhodes attained its pinnacle of power and brilliance, with its fame and wealth as a mercantile centre becoming known throughout the ancient world. The cause of this crowning achievement was the joint decision of the three cities to found a new trading centre at the northern tip of the island. The leaders of Ialysos, Cameiros and Lindos correctly judged that the future of the island lay in consolidation rather than decentralisation, especially with the increasing volume of trade now finding its way to the island. The city of Rhodes made its appearance as a newly planned settlement in 408 BC. Of the old cities, Ialysos and Cameiros gradually declined in importance, the former being described by Strabo, in the first century AD, as a mere hamlet. Lindos, however, was too valuable a fortress, in face of the Persian danger, to be neglected, and too useful a port of call. It remained a considerable town for a number of centuries after the foundation of Rhodes.

The new city was laid out in a carefully planned checkerboard pattern (Fig 10) and tradition attributes it to Hippodamus, though this is extremely doubtful. Hippodamus was the famous classical architect-planner who was responsible for the rebuilding of his own native city, Miletus, in accordance with

49

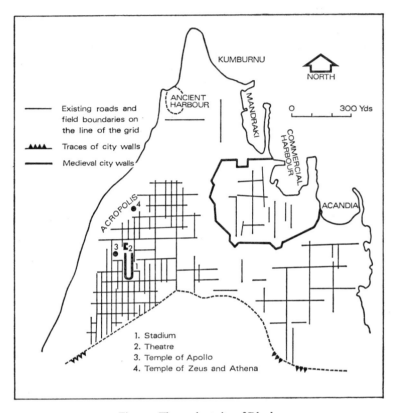

Fig 10   The ancient city of Rhodes

preconceived and regulated planning theories. According to
Aristotle he 'invented the method of partitioning cities and also
laid out Piraeus with intersecting streets'. Strabo speaks of him
as having planned Rhodes, but adds doubtfully, 'as they say'.
It seems unlikely that Hippodamus took any part in the design
of Rhodes for he was born around 500 BC and even if he was
alive in 408 BC his great age would certainly have prevented
him from taking an active part in its development. Moreover,
Rhodes was founded immediately after the revolt of the island
against the rule of Athens and it is unlikely that Hippodamus,

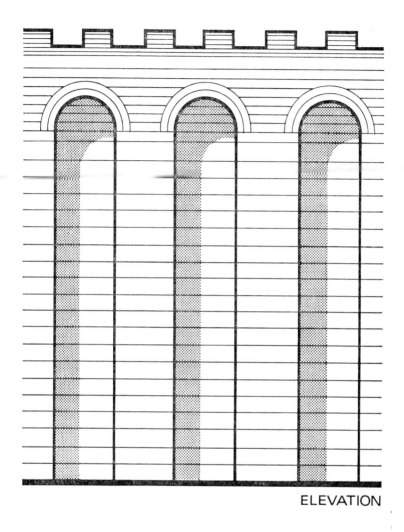

ELEVATION

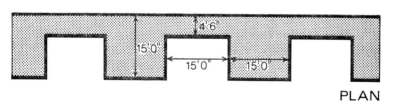

PLAN

Fig 11   Rhodes, the ancient walls

a staunch friend of Athens, would have offered his services to the enemy. Towards the end of the fifth century BC checkerboard plans were not unusual, especially when a new city had to be planned. Without doubt the Piraeus scheme and its author had become famous and it was probably usual to refer to it in a general manner as the 'Hippodamian way'. Without any deliberate intention, a tradition probably developed that both Piraeus and Rhodes were the work of Hippodamus.

The decision to build a new city as the capital of the unified island is of considerably greater interest than the speculation on whether Hippodamus was responsible for its design. Rhodes was built to accommodate around 100,000 inhabitants and it covered an area that was five or six times the size of the later medieval city. It had eight miles of landward walls and an important development in military architecture occurred with the construction of these fortifications (Fig 11). On the sides towards the city, the walls formed an arcade of tall arches vaulted a few feet below the wall-walk. The arched recesses were 15ft wide by 10ft 6in deep and were spaced 15ft apart. The portion of the wall at the back of the recess was 4ft 6in thick and the full thickness of the wall was 15ft. This scientific method of construction was followed later by the Romans and Byzantines. It had a number of advantages: a great saving of material; the arches were useful for the accommodation of troops; if breached, the damage was localised and its repair facilitated.

Rhodes was also equipped with five harbours that were partially or wholly artificial. Three of the basins were of capacious size and were formed out of indentations on the more sheltered eastern side of the cape (Fig 10). Adjoining their elaborate works was a large and complex naval yard protected by a strict security system. The magnificence of the city's harbours made Rhodes the best-equipped port in the Aegean and inspired Timosthenes to write a treatise *On Harbours* which filled the place held now by *The Mediterranean Pilot*.

Since World War II archaeologists have learned a great deal

Page 53 The village of Lindos, a highly compacted settlement of narrow streets and
flat-roofed houses

Page 54 Vegetation: (*above*) eroded hills and cultivated fields viewed from Mount Philerimos; (*below*) typical lowland vegetation of cacti, pines and wild fruit trees

about the city plan of ancient Rhodes. Aerial photography, air bombardment and, more recently, the rapid development of the town for tourist accommodation has revealed more evidence. Prior to the war, active excavation was undertaken by the Italians, and their archaeological plan of the city, published in 1936, recorded thirty-four classical and Hellenistic finds within the city's medieval walls. But the westward suburbs, rising steeply to the acropolis, Monte Smith, provide better evidence for the street grid and for ancient buildings. On the acropolis, excavations undertaken between 1916 and 1929 revealed the foundations of temples dedicated to Zeus and Athena Polias together with a stadium, a small theatre, a gymnasium, and a temple to Apollo. The complete site dates from the second century BC and the theatre, now completely restored, was probably an auditorium for the music and games associated with the cult of Apollo.

Bradford and Kondis, using aerial photographs, have traced a significant part of the street pattern of the ancient city (Fig 10). It closely resembled fifth-century Miletus which also covered a promontory in a similar street layout. In Rhodes the units of division averaged about 105yd long by 55yd wide and it seems probable that units of stadia (600 Greek ft, the equivalent of about 202yd) were used as the original basis of subdivision. The rectilinear plan with its uniform houses and thoroughfares was famous for retaining its decorative aspect from every visible angle and the 3,000 statues with which the city was adorned included the highly accomplished products of the Rhodian School. According to contemporary accounts the result was a city more spacious and decorative than any in the Greek world, with the exceptions of Athens and Syracuse.

POLITICS AND ECONOMICS

Rhodes quickly attained the position of being one of the leading maritime powers of the age and a carefully engineered political

D

and economic policy attempted to preserve its prosperity amidst the quarrels of the Greek city states. Where possible Rhodes endeavoured to maintain a neutral and independent position, and reserved judgement on political matters. The island trusted in a fleet so powerful and skilful that it was famous in ancient times. It guarded the narrow channel between the island and the mainland and the navy carried out a firm policy of supporting freedom of the seas and preserving the balance of power between one imperialist and another. But, from time to time, this enviable neutrality was broken, and a choice was often forced upon the island. Always the Rhodians chose with an eye to the main chance, their ultimate objective being to obtain independence.

The island's prosperity received impetus from the conquests of Alexander the Great which were to play an important role in the history of Hellenism. Rhodes was quick to see the advantages of siding with Macedonia and their combined forces succeeded in destroying the rival trading city of Tyre. Further Macedonian conquests gave Rhodes unrestricted access to Cyprus, Cicilia, Syria and Egypt. It appears that Alexander had a great admiration for Rhodes and helped to promote it commercially. When the city of Alexandria was founded in 331 BC, Alexander proved his admiration by adopting a system of government based on that of Rhodes, and the island opposite the harbour he named Antirodos.

Although Rhodes adjusted its political policies with considerable deftness, it became inevitably involved in the rivalries of succession following the death of Alexander in 323 BC. For a few years a central authority was maintained in the empire, but the lack of a capable royal successor resulted in political power devolving on the generals in the provinces. In little more than a decade these generals had become kings of warring states. Ptolemy created a Greek kingdom in Egypt and Seleucus in Asia with its capital first at Seleucia, then at Antioch. Cassander controlled Macedon and maintained sovereignty over the city states of Greece, Lysimachus held Thrace and Antigonus governed Syria and Anatolia. Of all the rulers only Antigonus had the will to restore the unity of the empire and with the advantages of a central position and the command of the sea he was able to seduce the Hellenic League of the Greek mainland from its allegiance to Cassander. He also promoted a new league for the Aegean islands and only Rhodes was strong enough to ignore it. Under Alexander, Rhodes had obtained a wide mainland protectorate in south-west Anatolia and the island made common cause with the Greek kings of Pergamum to resist Macedonian and Syrian aggression and to maintain the freedom of the seas and the independence of the Aegean city states. Antigonus' failure to disguise his ultimate ambition caused his enemies to combine against him and in the critical Battle of Ipsus (301 BC), Seleucus took Syria and Cicilia, Lysimachus gained Anatolia and Ptolemy acquired Palestine and Cyprus. Rhodes retained its independence.

THE SIEGE OF DEMETRIUS

Prior to the Battle of Ipsus, Antigonus had solicited an alliance with Rhodes against the Egyptian Ptolemy. The Rhodians, refusal was on perfectly logical grounds as trade with Egypt played too large a part in the economy of the island. With the dismemberment of Alexander's empire the island's strongest political and economic ties were with Egypt and the island became a depot for the export of goods from Alexandria, chiefly spices. In 305 BC, Demetrius (surnamed Poliorcetes or 'Besieger'), the son of Antigonus, launched his great attack on Rhodes.

As a general, Demetrius was considered a candidate for the honours of a second Alexander and he launched his siege on Rhodes at the height of his military career and with an army specialised in assaults on heavily fortified positions. It is reported that his forces numbered 40,000 men, excluding cavalry, sailors and engineers. They were carried on 170 troopships, convoyed by 200 men-of-war and by countless ships with provisions and smaller vessels which followed him in the hope of chance of spoil. The Rhodian forces numbered 6,000 citizens and 1,000 aliens within the city, but the slaves were also armed for the siege and it is estimated that they alone must have added some 16,000 men to the standing garrison. Further reinforcements came from Crete and Egypt and on the eve of the battle it was the case of some 25,000 men besieged by roughly twice that number.

Demetrius was equipped with a wide range of sophisticated war weapons, including assault towers and giant catapults but his most dreaded weapon was the Helepolis. This was a nine-storey assault tower on wheels of oak that dwarfed the Rhodian walls. It was replete with catapults, grappling irons and draw-bridges which could disgorge its infantry upon the parapets and it appears it took an operational force of 3,400 men to propel it. The whole structure was given a tough outer skin of plaited osiers and hides and the top floor was a nest for archers. There is some argument about the original size of the Helepolis. Diodorus claims it was 50m high by 25m broad and Vitruvius calculated its weight at 125 tons.

The Helepolis caused extensive damage to the city's fortifications, but the Rhodians showed little signs of weakening and the enemy was repeatedly driven back. The siege, which lasted a year, was abruptly terminated when Demetrius received a message from Antigonus ordering him to conclude a truce with the Rhodians and to return. The treaty, which was not un-favourable to Rhodes, guaranteed the island's freedom in exchange for an alliance with Antigonus against any enemy with the exception of Egypt. Either out of sheer necessity, or as a mark of respect for the Rhodians, Demetrius left all the equipment he had brought for the siege, including the Helepolis. According to tradition Demetrius asked that it should be sold and from the proceeds a statue to commemorate the victory was to be erected. This was the Colossus of Rhodes, the statue of Helios the sun god.

THE COLOSSUS

The building of the statue was undertaken by Chares of Lindos, a pupil of Lysippus. Work on it began in 302 BC and it cost the sculptor 12 years of his life to cast and mould. It was fashioned in bronze and measured 70 cubits in height (something over 35m). The precise site of the colossus remains a mystery, as does the pose, for it was never described by reliable eye-witnesses. It came to be regarded as the protector of Rhodes and served as a landmark for vessels arriving from all quarters, but the theory that it straddled the entrance to the harbour is a medieval confection. The spread of the legs in a figure of that height could hardly have been more than 8m and although ships were then small and masts could be lowered to sail under the statue, a site at the back of Rhodes city, towards Monte Smith, would seem more probable. Also, when it was over-thrown, it appears that the great statue fell on the land.

The colossus was placed in the catalogue of the seven wonders of the ancient world and it stood for 60-odd years. It was des-troyed by earthquake in 227 BC and for centuries it lay in ruin in the city it had adorned. According to legend, Helios was believed to have been displeased with the statue and his oracle forbade its restoration. No Rhodian would touch it and it lay for nearly 900 years until AD 635 when the remains were trans-ported piece by piece to the Levant by Saracen marauders and then sold to Jewish merchants. Tradition has it that 900 camels were used for this purpose—an extraordinary large caravan for the transportation of what would amount to roughly twenty tons of metal! An equally romantic addendum is that Rhodes got its colossus back in the form of Turkish cannonballs during the famous siege of AD 1522.

THE TRIUMPH OF HELLENISM

Interwoven with the political tale of division and decline following the death of Alexander the Great is a success story revolving around the economic and cultural triumph of Hellenism. In this Rhodes played a major role as its position in relation to the great trading cities of the eastern and western Mediterranean gave it exceptional commercial advantages (Fig 12). The major commercial centres of the East were Alexandria and Antioch, the former having grown rapidly under the Hellenising influences of the Ptolemies. An urban and economic revival also occurred along the Aegean coast of Asia Minor with its important trading centres of Ephesus, Smyrna, Nicaea and Pergamum. In the western basin the great economic and demographic centre was Rome itself.

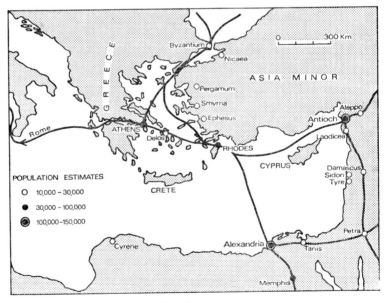

Fig 12   Hellenistic trade routes

Rhodes lay at the focal point on the trading routes linking these cities and all items of Mediterranean trade passed through the island—ivory, spices, gold, resin, silver, copper, tin, furs, glass, textiles, linen, wheat, timber, wine, oil, fish, amber, iron, wool, pottery, mercury, papyrus and metalwork. The biggest export was wine. Rhodian amphorae, found all over the Mediterranean and adjoining areas, attest to the wideness of this trade. When the earthquake devastated the city and its economy in 227 BC, the worth of Rhodes as a necessary centre of Mediterranean trade can be gauged from the gifts of money and food presented to the island by her allies, particularly Egypt. This was a demonstration of the commercial solidarity of the Greek world and its faith in Rhodes. The island quickly recovered and in 170 BC Polybius mentions the sum of one million drachmae accruing to Rhodes from the levy of a 2 per cent import and export duty. In the field of international banking and exchange Rhodes was a key city of Hellenistic commerce and although bills of exchange did not operate, letters of credit were known.

The government of the city seems to have been a limited democracy, or perhaps rather an aristocracy, under which power rested with the leading families. Its population was cosmopolitan, but Rhodes never had internal troubles and could in an emergency, as with the siege of Demetrius, arm its slaves. The Rhodian fleet probably never exceeded fifty ships, but its quality was considered the best in the ancient world. The city was prominent in shipbuilding advances, for which the age was famous, and riggings and steering-gears were improved and the new bowsprit sail made the navigation of large craft easier. The island's code of maritime law was equally famous and was subsequently adopted by the Antonines. Fragments of it were also embedded in the Byzantine compilation, *Rhodian Sea Law*, and thence passed to Venice. The Sea Law regulated commercial navigation and included the Law of Jettison, dealing with the division of losses between the owner of the ship and the owners of the cargo in cases where part of the cargo had to be abandoned to save the vessel. The law fixed the liability for the safety of the ship and cargo on the ship-owner, the lessee merchants and the passengers. In case of storm or piracy, they were all expected to make good the losses. These provisions were intended to serve as a sort of insurance.

INTELLECTUAL METROPOLIS

It is not surprising that such a rich and flourishing city developed into a major centre for Greek learning and a home for schools of sculpture, painting, literature, oratory and philosophy. The Rhodian victory over Demetrius furthered its status as an intellectual capital and it rivalled Alexandria and Pergamum as a leader in the sciences and the liberal arts. In Hellenistic times Rhodes was one of the main schools of Greek sculpture, along with Pergamum and Ephesus, and it long remained a university.

A thriving school of sculpture was established as early as the sixth century BC and the foundation of the city of Rhodes brought an influx of artists from all over the Greek world. Although the names of various sculptors are known from inscriptions on statueless plinths, the few statues actually found in Rhodes are unsigned. Much of our knowledge of early Rhodian sculptors comes from Pindar, who was impressed by their technical skill and by the life and vigour of their products. It is reported that when the city was at its zenith of prosperity there were at least 3,000 statues adorning its streets and buildings, many of them colossi.

One of the great sculptors of the fourth century was Lysippus who founded the School of Rhodes. He produced the famous *Chariot of the Sun God*. Another statue to the god, found at Delphi, and the horses adorning the front of St Mark's Cathedral, Venice, are also attributed to him. Chares of Lindos, the creator of the colossus was a pupil of Lysippus. Other leaders of the school included Protogenes, Bryaxis, Pythocritos and Aristonides. Some of the products of Rhodian sculpture, including the *Aphrodite of Rhodes*, the *Marine Venus* and the *Sun God* are in the Museum of Rhodes, others are in collections scattered throughout the world.

The work of Rhodian painters has long since vanished but descriptions by classical and Hellenistic writers indicate that painting had reached a high level of development early in the history of the island. Its peak was reached with the partnership of Protogenes and Apelles and Pliny records their meeting and subsequent careers. The portrait of Ialysos, the mythical creator of that city, was one of the more important works of Protogenes, as were portraits of Philiskos the poet, the god Pan, an unknown athlete, and the mother of Aristotle.

In Hellenistic times Rhodes could boast more than seventy poets, historians, philosophers and orators and its spiritual and artistic achievement earned the island the title of 'a second Athens—a storehouse of knowledge and a fertile ground for men of intellect'. Famous poets, either natives or settlers, included Antagoras, Pesinous, Apollonios, Evodos, Timachidas, Semias and Temocreon. People travelled from all parts of the ancient world to study oratory and to listen to the great masters such as Aeschines, Poseidonios, Meneclis, Vion and Molon. Among the leading Roman names to attend the Rhodian School were Caesar, Brutus, Anthony, Cassius, Tiberius and Cicero.

THE ROMANS

Into the complicated world of the 'successor' states of Alexander's empire the Romans were drawn unwittingly by the hostility of Philip V of Macedon and the appeals of the Greek city states for protection. Egypt also asked for assistance against the aggression of Syria. Roman intervention in eastern Mediterranean affairs began around 200 BC and had severe repercussions on Rhodes. It threatened the commercial and political integrity of the island. In the struggles which followed, the Romans liberated the Greek city states and leagues from Macedonian control (196 BC), repelled the Syrian invasion of Egypt (192–1 BC) and, aided by the fleets of Rhodes and Pergamum, deprived Syria of its possessions north of the Taurus. With the weight of Rome behind them, Pergamum was to hold the Asia Minor peninsula and the Aegean against Macedon, and Rhodes was to hold Syria to its treaty limits on the Cicilian shore.

Initially, Rome was indifferent to its obligations incurred in the East and its reluctance to impose a system of provincial administration brought about chaos. Following a needless quarrel in 167 BC Rome intervened in the Rhodian policy of suppressing piracy and revoked the grant to Rhodes of the Asia Minor provinces of Lycia and Caria. By 164 BC a reversal of Roman policy had taken place and the old kingdoms were converted into provinces. Not content with depriving Rhodes of its political independence the Romans also impaired the island's commercial freedom. For some time Rome had regarded Rhodes' flourishing commerce with envy, and to divert trade away from the island, Delos in the Cyclades was declared a free port. Delos quickly took its place as the centre of international transit in the Aegean and the destruction of the trading city of Corinth in 146 gave it further opportunity for expansion. This was a fatal blow to Rhodian commerce and its annual revenue of one million drachmae from harbour taxes fell to 15,000 drachmae. The final blow to Rhodian power was an unheralded attack by Cassius in 42 BC who stripped, burned and butchered the city in reprisal for Rhodes' refusal to join him against his enemies on the death of Julius Caesar.

Under Anthony and Augustus part of Rhodes' insular domain was restored and the island took on a new administrative function. Augustus confirmed its former status as a 'free and allied city' and Vespasian made it the capital of a new 'province of the islands'. This was subordinated later to Diocletian's 'province of Asia' (AD 284–305) and was included in the Byzantine *thema* of Cibyra—maritime south-west Asia Minor from Miletus to Seleucia.

4   MEDIEVAL RHODES

A S Rhodes entered into the medieval world a somewhat similar set of circumstances faced the island: geographical position and strategic importance were again to rule its destiny. Whereas, in antiquity, the island was inevitably involved in the wars of city states and kingdoms, it was now caught up in the web of intrigue and conflict between the rising sea powers of Italy and the Byzantine Empire, while on a broader canvas it was intimately involved in the religious and political problems between the Moslem East and western Christendom.

When the Roman Empire was subdivided for military and administrative convenience, Rhodes naturally became part of the eastern section and exchanged the rule of Rome for that of Byzantium. For some time the Roman emperors had felt the need for a new administrative centre and under Diocletian (AD 284–305) eastern and western sections were established in line with the division between Latin- and Greek-speaking populations. Diocletian took up residence in the East, at Nicomedia, near the Sea of Marmara. Early in the next century Constantine reunited the two halves, but fixed the capital in the East and the ancient Greek city of Byzantium was enlarged to form Constantinople, the 'New Rome'. When the empire was again divided, what had started as an administrative partition became after AD 395 a more fundamental separation. Where one emperor had formerly ruled at Rome, now two imperial colleagues, ruling jointly, shared the burdens of government. In the West one emperor resided at Rome, Milan,

66

Ravenna or Trèves, while in the East, Antioch, but chiefly Constantinople, became the capitals. The western part of the empire collapsed under the assaults of barbarian invaders, but the eastern section continued as a permanent factor amidst the changing political fortunes of Europe and the Moslem East, lasting in some form or other until it was destroyed by the Ottoman Turks in the fifteenth century. The Roman Empire of the East, or as it was alternatively called, the Byzantine Empire, was characterised by both Greek and Roman traditions. In language, literature and theology, Greek influence was paramount; in law, diplomacy and military tradition it relied on Roman experience.

Although the concept of Byzantium long remained, from a geographical standpoint the empire was a continually changing expression, and despite periods of vitality and reconquest its frontiers tended to recede. In the East it was constantly threatened by the political expansion of Persia, and in the South the Arabs, spiritually and politically united by Mohammed, proved an even greater danger. Between AD 637 and 649 the Arabs succeeded in subjugating Persia and established a caliphate embracing Egypt, Syria and the eastern frontiers of Asia Minor. In the eighth and ninth centuries the Umayyad and Abbasid Caliphates increased their control of the Near East at the expense of Byzantium though Asia Minor was held until c 1100 when the Seljuk Turks conquered most of the interior and created a sultanate with its capital at Iconium.

Throughout the early part of the Byzantine period Rhodes failed to distinguish itself in either commerce or in the arts and sciences: in fact it never recovered the prosperity and prestige which it had enjoyed in the Mediterranean world prior to the rise of Rome. Within the Byzantine Empire, as under Roman rule, Rhodes and the rest of Greece enjoyed only provincial status. The sea which in classical and Hellenistic times had offered a fertile field for commercial exploitation, became increasingly a source of danger. With an insignificant fleet and a town often severely damaged by earthquakes the island was easy plunder for the Goths, Persians, Saracens, Arabs and Turks. Fortresses at Lindos, Cameiros, Skala, Feraclos, Philerimos, and elsewhere, were the direct result of Byzantium's attempts to fend off these constant threats.

VENETIANS AND GENOESE

With the advent of the Crusades Rhodes was economically revived and functioned as a supply station on the route to the Holy Land. In 1097 Rhodian ships carried supplies to Crusading armies and in 1191 Richard Coeur de Lion stayed in Rhodes with his English fleet. This example was followed by Philip of France on his return from the Holy Land. Realisation of the island's important position made it an attractive prize for the developing commercial states of Western Europe. Venice was the first to acquire special privileges in Rhodes which were granted by the Byzantine Emperor Alexios Comnenos in 1082. This resulted in the virtual domination of the island by the Venetians, and on the death of the emperor the privileges were rescinded. When, during the Fourth Crusade, the Byzantine throne was overthrown and Constantinople was sacked by the Franks (1204), the empire witnessed the parcelling out of its Aegean possessions among the Italian states best able to exploit them. Genoa held Naxos, Mytilene and Chios, Venice secured Crete, but Rhodes remained independent under a Greek governor. This was Leo Gavalla, who soon after 1204 had styled himself 'Dominus Rhode et Cicladum insularum, Ksserus Leo Gavalla' (Lord of Rhodes and the Cyclades, Caesar Leo Gavalla) and had cast off all but a semblance of allegiance to Byzantium. Rhodes was regarded as a pirate state which might justifiably be attacked without the leave of Byzantium. When Venice opened hostilities against the island, Gavalla was unable to defend it with his own forces. In 1234 an alliance granted Venice vast commercial privileges but returned Rhodes to the Byzantine Empire.

Throughout the thirteenth century possession of the island was hotly contested by the Genoese and Venetians. In 1261, Genoa gained the advantage over its rival when Emperor Michael Palaeologos signed a treaty awarding it commercial supremacy in the Levant. It was largely as a result of the connivance of Genoa, together with the moral and financial support of Pope Clement V, that Rhodes was again wrested from Byzantium and given to the Knights of St John, together with adjacent islands in the south-east Aegean. A Genoese adventurer, Vignole di Vignoli, was already 'renting' Kos and Lemnos from the Emperor Andronicus II and the Knights contracted with him for a combined assault on Rhodes and any other islands that they could occupy. Rhodes was to be handed over to the Order and Kos and Lemnos were to be ceded to it by Vignoli. In a shaming deal revenues were to be divided one-third to Vignoli and two-thirds to the Knights. The initial parties landed in July 1307, but by the end of September only Philerimos had fallen. On 5 September, Pope Clement V confirmed the Knights in their possession of Rhodes but it was a further two years before they were to secure complete control of the island.

THE KNIGHTS OF ST JOHN

The Knightly Order of St John of Jerusalem was one of the three great military orders which sprang out of the Crusades, the other two being the Templars and the Teutonic Order. They had been forced out of Palestine following the losses to the Arabs of their possessions at Krak des Chevaliers and Acre. For a brief period they settled in Cyprus. The possession of Rhodes gave them for the first time full territorial sovereignty and they were quick to recognise the island as a suitable location for a permanent base from which to contest the Moslem advance. Papal interest in establishing the Knights on Rhodes stemmed from both practical and political considerations—the advantage of having a militant body of Christians in a place where they could do maximum damage to the Moslem enemy, and where they could be of little trouble to Catholic Christendom. The main reason for the Genoese support was commercial.

The Order had evolved from a hospice founded by Italian merchants in the eleventh century. Its initial purpose was the succouring and lodging of Christian pilgrims on their way to the holy places of Jerusalem which were then in the Caliphate of Egypt. The hospice was dedicated to St John the Baptist and the monks attached to it were known as the Frères Hospitallers de St Jean de Jerusalem. Following the success of the First Crusade, the Hospitallers transformed themselves, as did their rivals the Templars, into a military order, extending their protective role, but still continuing with their nursing and sheltering duties. The rules of the new order were confirmed by Pope Pascal II in 1113, from which time the Knights received benefices from estates donated to it in Europe.

The prime objective of the Order now became the defence of the church against the Moslem 'infidel' and members were required to make three fundamental vows of chastity, obedience and poverty. To enter the Order as a prospective Knight, a youth had to prove himself to be of unblemished, noble and Catholic parentage and an exhaustive enquiry was made into each postulant's eligibility. A noble could be admitted at the age of fourteen and enjoy the privileges of residing in the fortress and wearing the full dress of the Order. The admission of full privilege to arms, however, could not be confirmed before the age of eighteen. The youthfulness of the Knights was remarkable and so great were the dangers and hardships of the life they had chosen, hardly one Knight in twenty lived to reach the age of fifty.

On their arrival in Rhodes the Order had settled into three classes: the Knights militant, recruited only from noble

Page 71   Windmill irrigation near the village of Trianda. Water is especially important for citrus cultivation

Page 72   (*above*) The temple of Apollo on the ancient acropolis of Rhodes; (*below*) the ancient city of Cameiros, the Pompeii of Rhodes

families; the serving brothers who made up a corps of assistants
and nurses; and the chaplains and almoners who attended to
religious matters. The Knights were grouped according to
their country of origin into *langues* or 'tongues'—Provence,
Auvergne, France, Italy, Spain, Germany and England. The
official language was French and manuscripts were written in
Latin. Each 'tongue' had its official headquarters, known as an
inn, which was under the command of a bailiff. The bailiffs,
collectively, constituted the Chapter of the Order, presided over
by the grand master who was elected by the Knights for life.
From 1310 to 1522 the Order was served by a total of nineteen
grand masters (see Appendix B), the majority of whom were
French. French Knights were always in an overwhelming
majority as not only were there Knights of France, but also
French-speaking Knights of the 'tongues' of Auvergne and
Provence. However, in 1377 a Spaniard was elected as grand
master with a tenure which lasted nineteen years. Both his
successors were also Spanish and the latter, Antoine Flavian
(1421–37), took steps to increase Spanish influence by sub-
dividing the 'tongue' of Spain into the 'tongues' of Castile and
Aragon. This was a significant step in the organisation of the
Hospitallers as voting in the councils was based not upon the
number of Knights but upon the number of nations present.

In addition to the three classes outlined above, the Order also
required officers for its fleet and army, together with admini-
strators for the numerous estates it owned throughout Europe.
The suppression of the Templars by the Papacy and the French
monarchy in 1310–12 also resulted in their wealth and possessions passing to the Knights. Great suspicion had been cast on
the Templars' morality and Crusading enthusiasm, leaning
further as they did towards a semi-secular organisation with
their own private policies. Moreover, they had become pioneers
in international banking in medieval Europe, thereby alienating
their brotherhood from its initial vow of poverty. The Hospitallers' estates were grouped into commanderies, bailiwicks and

E

priories and by the beginning of the sixteenth century no less than 656 commanderies existed in Europe. These estates financed the military and social operations of the Knights and at all Christian courts permanent embassies were maintained.

A great deal of romantic sentiment is conjured up by the Knights, the Crusades and the Age of Chivalry. Perhaps it should be stressed that the whole concept sowed such hate in the East that avenging counter-Crusades were to bring Moslem forces to the gates of Vienna. The Order, which began as a nursing brotherhood, became aggressively military and Rhodes developed into a naval power of aristocratic corsairs. They laudably maintained their hospital, though for their own kind, and it was the knightly patients, not the islanders, who ate from silver plates.

THE FORTIFICATIONS

Once established on Rhodes, the Knights' preoccupation was the continuation of warfare against the 'infidel'—by raids on the coasts of Asia Minor and Syria. Protected to the north, south and rear by Genoa and Venice, the island became a powerful member of the Frankish hegemony over Greek seas. The Knights took the precaution of protecting themselves from the east by establishing fortress bases on neighbouring islands —Simi, Nisiros, Tilos, Kos, Kalimnos, Leros, Chalki, Alimnia, Kastellorizzo—as well as the great fortress of St Peter, Budrum, on the Asiatic mainland (Fig 13). Allied with Cyprus, Venice and Genoa, the Knights attacked Smyrna in 1344 and succeeded in its capture in 1348. An assault on Alexandria followed in 1365 and abortive attempts on Tarsus, Tripoli and Latakia in 1367.

On Rhodes the Knights were impressed by the defensive possibilities of the acropolis of Lindos and crowned it with a stronghold. Elsewhere on the island they erected, or restored, some further thirty castles and strong points, notably at Paradission, Castello, Monolithos, Lardos, Asklepion, Feraclos and

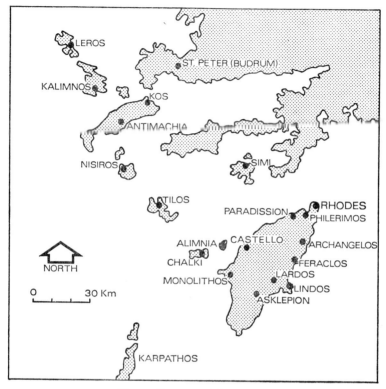

Fig 13   Fortresses of the Knights

Archangelos. Watchtowers around the whole coast were kept manned and a primitive semaphore and carrier-pigeon by day and signal fires by night ensured that alarms were relayed from fortress to fortress. The outlying islands each had their garrison and at least one dispatch vessel.

The main illustration of their art in defence and military prowess, however, comes from Rhodes town itself. The constant danger of attack by hostile neighbours laid upon the Knights the necessity of maintaining defences in a high state of readiness. The walls of the town with their succession of towers, bastions and barbicans are magnificent examples of the military archi-

75

tecture of the thirteenth, fourteenth and fifteenth centuries and are preserved almost intact throughout their 4km circuit. This preservation is due in part to the fact that under Turkish rule, as in the case of Constantinople, the lands immediately outside the walls came to be used as cemeteries. At Rhodes these cemeteries have now been converted to gardens from which the fortifications may be viewed to great advantage. The defences have been extensively studied by Gabriel who stressed in *The City of Rhodes* that their architectural and historical interest is increased by the fact that the various periods of construction are easily discernible from the arms of the grand masters built into them. Also the enceinte was gradually extended outwards rather than radically remodelled, which again makes study and dating easier. Rhodes was fortified during a period of change in the art of fortification and it illustrates the transition from the typical medieval pattern of main and outer walls with protecting towers, to the early forms of the modern bastion.

During the fourteenth century relatively modest defences were constructed, following in places Hellenistic and Byzantine foundations (Fig 14). The initial walls were between 2.75 and 3.7m in thickness and about 9m in height with crenellated parapets. They were punctuated at intervals by a series of towers, and the south and west sections, towards the land, were further

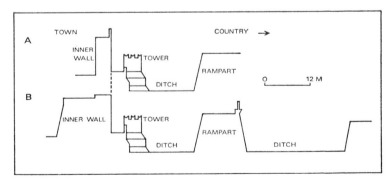

Fig 14 The medieval walls of Rhodes town (a) before and (b) after 1480

strengthened by ditches with a narrow berm. These fortifications presented essentially the old pre-gunpowder arrangement of high thin walls, towers and ditches. There were no bastions to provide flanking fire against attempted breaching of the walls, which was to become commoner than the old scaling attacks. The earliest-dated and extant towers are two on the northern side of the city between the towers of St Paul and St Peter. They bear the arms of Juan Fernandez Heredia of Aragon (Grand Master 1377–96) and are rectangular, purely medieval in bearing, and possess only cross-slits for the deployment of bows.

When the cannon became a universally used instrument of war and its potential fully recognised by the Turks in their assault and capture of Constantinople in 1453, the Knights were forced to devise new and more elaborate fortifications. Systematic improvements of obsolete defences were undertaken with the aid of European, chiefly Italian, engineers. Antonio Fluvian of Aragon (1421–37) added a number of towers to the enceinte, including St George's Tower in which provision for defence with guns made its first appearance in Rhodes. Enemy attacks were still directed primarily against curtain walls and one of the major steps was to reinforce the interior of old walls with earthen banks. Not only did this resist enemy bombardment, it also provided scope for the deployment of the defenders' own cannons. The total thickness of the walls was increased to about 12m. On the landward side ditches were widened and deepened and in places they were augmented by an outer rampart and second ditch. Many of the towers were lowered to the general height of the curtain walls and bulwarks were constructed to protect salient gateways and towers.

Much of this strengthening work and the construction of new defences was undertaken during the time of Grand Masters Orsini of Italy (1467–76) and d'Abusson of Auvergne (1476–1505) with the latter responsible for repairing the damage of the 1480 Moslem siege and an earthquake in the following year. Repairing and thickening of the main curtain was continued by

77

Emery d'Amboise of France (1505–12) and Fabrizio del Carretto of Italy (1513–21), but the last Grand Master of Rhodes, Philippe Villiers de l'Isle Adam of France (1521–2), had little time to improve defences before the Turks were upon him.

The original fortified circuit contained eight gates and although they were constantly being repaired, altered and rendered more difficult to attack, they nevertheless provided weak links in the city's defences. Two gates on the west, those of St George and St Athanasius, and the Gate of Italy on the south-west were later blocked for greater security. In the north-west, St Anthony's Gate was enclosed and a new one, the Amboise Gate was built in the outwork in 1504. This was one of the most complicated, and also monumental, of the defensive gates. It consisted of a bridge with three arches, spanning an outer moat which led to the main entrance located between massive cylindrical towers 12m in diameter. Within the thickness of the wall the vaulted road made an S-bend and passed through a second gate to a terreplein separated from the town by a third moat with further bridges and gates.

Another highly defensive entrance was the Koskinou or St John's Gate which was considerably strengthened under Raymond Zacosta of Aragon (1461–7) and finally completed around 1480 (Fig 15). It was protected by a series of earthworks, forming three tiers of battlements, and also by two ditches. The sinuous approach passage, causing assailants to change direction and expose themselves to flank attack, was interrupted in succession by two drawbridges. An outer moat with a stone bridge and drawbridge led to the first gate and a polygonal rampart that was provided with a gun platform with embrasures. A second moat and bridge led to the second rampart in the form of a spur with a square tower, to the right of which passed the road leading to the inner gate. A number of shields bear witness to the numerous changes and reconstructions of this gateway which must be considered as one of the most carefully built works of the defences.

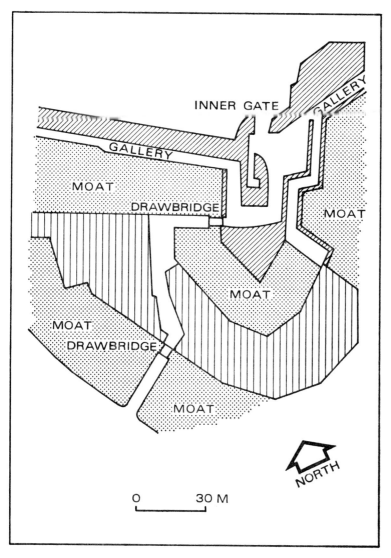

INNER GATE

GALLERY

GALLERY

MOAT

DRAWBRIDGE

MOAT

MOAT

MOAT

DRAWBRIDGE

MOAT

NORTH

0   30 M

Fig 15   The Koskinou Gate

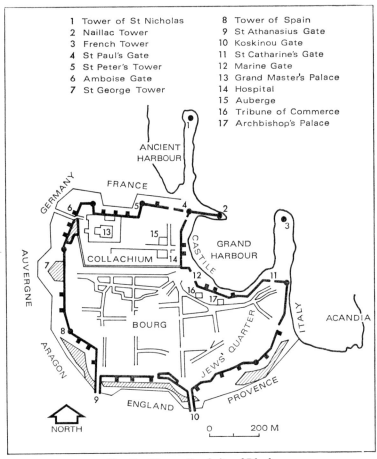

1	Tower of St Nicholas	8	Tower of Spain
2	Naillac Tower	9	St Athanasius Gate
3	French Tower	10	Koskinou Gate
4	St Paul's Gate	11	St Catharine's Gate
5	St Peter's Tower	12	Marine Gate
6	Amboise Gate	13	Grand Master's Palace
7	St George Tower	14	Hospital
		15	Auberge
		16	Tribune of Commerce
		17	Archbishop's Palace

Fig 16   The medieval city of Rhodes

When the city was placed in a state of siege each section of the enceinte was allocated to a 'tongue' for defence (Fig 16). France held the northern approach with Germany next, on the western flank; Auvergne and Aragon followed to the southwest; England held the southernmost section, with Provence on her eastern flank; Italy and Castile shared the seaward approaches. The Commercial Harbour was protected by two

80

moles between which a chain was stretched to restrict entry. On the northern mole was the 46m high Tower of Naillac, completed at the beginning of the fifteenth century. Its gun platform dominated the sea approaches from a height of 20m and the tower was a key point during the protracted siege of Suleiman. The French tower occupied the southernmost mole and commanded both the Commercial Harbour and the Bay of Acandia. North of the Commercial Harbour, the naval port of Mandraki was guarded by the bulky St Nicholas Fort, built around 1464 with funds supplied by Duke Philip of Burgundy. It was elaborately strengthened after the 1480 Turkish siege and took the form of an irregular-sided citadel with a tower rising from an inner keep—an independent fortress in its own right.

THE MEDIEVAL CITY

The fortified medieval city occupied only part of the harbour quarter of the Hellenistic settlement. It was disposed in a rough semi-circle around the Commercial Harbour and was subdivided by a low internal wall which separated the Collachium, or Knights' convent proper, from the merchants' town or Bourg. The enclosed Collachium (Fig 17) occupied an area roughly 360m long by 250m wide and housed the grand master's palace, the inns of the 'tongues', the hospital and all the administrative buildings of the Holy Religion. Within it, also, was the Conventual Church of St John the Baptist, patron and protector of the Order.

The palace, now completely restored, stood at the highest point in the city on the site of an ancient temple to Apollo, and it dominated the whole Collachium. The imposing citadel, built on a rectangular plan and bordered by towers was completed at the end of the fourteenth century and repaired after the earthquake of 1481. It constituted a fortress within itself from which communication could be made with the ramparts

81

of the city. To withstand siege it was designed with underground storerooms including two silos for pressing wheat. In times of peace the palace-citadel served as the residence of the grand master and as the place of assembly for the Order.

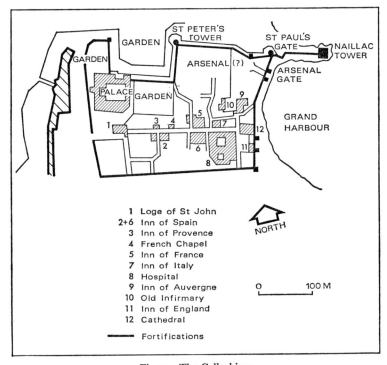

Fig 17 The Collachium

The main thoroughfare of the Collachium, popularly called 'the Street of the Knights', linked the citadel with the port via a defended gate. It was 200m long by 6m wide and was lined with the medieval inns which housed the Knights and in which meetings were held and guests entertained. The Italians carried out discreet restoration work on the thoroughfare and, today, it represents one of the most remarkable survivals of a medieval street in Europe. At the port end of the street stood the hospital which was one of the largest of the medieval buildings and symbolised the original mission of the Order. It was founded in 1437 by Grand Master Fluvian (1421–37) and was completed around 1490 after work was interrupted by Turkish siege. A great hall, measuring 50m by 11m, occupied the eastern wing of the upper floor of the hospital. This served as the infirmary and it is reported that its patients were served food on gold and silver plates. The hall could accommodate up to one hundred patients and to the east was a small Gothic chapel. The hospital was complete with another large chamber, which served as a dining-room for its personnel, and with numerous small dressing-rooms and storerooms.

The merchants' quarter was also a well-planned area and contained many impressive buildings, including the palace of the Latin archbishop, the Commercial Courts, the Greek Orthodox Cathedral and the Church of St Mary. Its main functions, however, were trading and manufacturing and it was orientated towards the commercial harbour with which it communicated via the Marine and St Catharine's Gates.

The native Rhodians were generally loyal to the Knights, but they appear to have had little political power and were rarely among the wealthier classes. Society was a Latin-Greek amalgam and the city was dominated by an indispensable colonial element of traders, bankers, shipbuilders, architects, engineers, lawyers and craftsmen. The majority had emigrated from Spain, Italy and France, and in some cases from Germany and England. The south-eastern section of the city housed a large Jewish colony whose numbers were considerably increased as the result of the Jewish expulsion from Spain during the sixteenth century. The Jews developed their traditional interests in textiles, services, trade and money-lending. These lay subjects of the Order were always a minority, outnumbered by the indigenous Greeks who formed the peasant and artisan classes and who were firmly restricted to subordinate roles under Hospitaller rule.

The Knights exacted tribute from the islanders in the form of taxes, duties, food requisitions and labour recruitment. The latter formed the foundation upon which the acclaimed military engineering feats of the Knights rested. In many ways the population was forcefully subjected and Greek participation in the politics and administration of the island was fostered only in the face of Ottoman attacks. The performance by the Greeks of minor functions in island administration began during the rule of Grand Master Zacosta (1461–7).

During the initial period of Hospitaller rule the security and political stability generated a rapid increase in commercial activity and Rhodes and Simi became important shipping centres. But the effects of the Knights on the landscape of the island had both positive and negative results. Most serious in the long run was the rapid depletion of local timber supplies for shipbuilding. Furthermore, the impressive commercial gains were quickly dissipated in the wake of destructive Ottoman attacks and Moslem pirates.

THE MOSLEM CAMPAIGNS

Throughout the fifteenth century the Moslem threat to Rhodes loomed large, especially as piecemeal conquest of the Aegean islands isolated the Knights from their western allies. Smyrna was retaken by the Turks in 1412, Genoa lost Chios in 1415 and the straits to the Sea of Marmara were strongly defended, barring the way to Constantinople and the rich trading centres of the Black Sea. In spite of their cultural ties with Rhodes, Venice, Genoa and Florence had only their trading interests at heart when dealing with the Turks and often they were reluctant to aid the Knights in their assaults on the Turkish mainland. The Italian states were often positive enemies, for in 1311 the Genoese bribed the Turks to attack Rhodes in reprisal for the Knights' interference in their specialised trade in Egyptian slaves.

The first Moslem attacks on Rhodes took place during the period of Grand Master Jean de Lastic (1437–54). The Egyptian conquest of Cyprus whetted the sultan's appetite for subjugating Rhodes, which for long had been a thorn in the side of the Islamic Empire. On three occasions the Egyptians attempted to reduce the island, but on each occasion their efforts were frustrated by the valiance and readiness of the Knights. The first campaign occurred in the summer of 1440 when a fleet of fifteen ships sailed from the Nile to Rhodes by way of Cyprus and Alaya in Asia Minor in order to obtain reinforcements. The Knights were able to intercept the Mamluk landing in time, but preparation for a new assault on the island began in 1442. Approximately one year later a fleet carrying 1,500 regular troops and a large number of volunteers sailed from Egypt, again via eastern Mediterranean ports. Delays, however, and the approach of winter, prevented them reaching Rhodes and after sacking the small island fortress of Kastellorizzo they retired to Egypt. The third campaign was mounted early in 1444 but in spite of 1,000 Mamluks and a body of 18,000 recruits it turned out to be as luckless as its predecessors. The siege lasted forty days and ended in a sea battle in which the Knights were victorious.

The Egyptian attacks emphasised the strong military organisation of the Knights and their rigorous observance of discipline in the ranks. Moreover they had developed a closely knit system of international espionage, an intelligence service unique in medieval times, whereby agents in hostile countries forewarned the grand master of any military movement against the island. Thus the Order was always ready to repulse surprise attacks. A landing on Rhodes at the Bay of Malona did succeed in sacking the fortresses of Malona and Archangelos, but for the next twenty-three years Rhodes was able to take, and hold, the initiative at sea. Moslem forces, however, continued to mount ever-increasing assaults on the other islands of the Aegean and although attacks on Kos, Simi and Nisiros in 1457 were beaten off, the Order's fleet was unable to save the northern islands of Lemnos, Thasos and Lesbos.

MOHAMMED THE CONQUEROR

Following the series of victories over Egypt the prestige of the Knights was considerably enhanced. Throughout Europe opinion began to move towards a complacent myth of the invincibility of Rhodes and a wishful conviction that it was under special divine protection. Egypt, however, had established a dangerous precedent for its Ottoman successors, who twice besieged the island and finally inflicted an inexorable disaster upon the Knights.

Between the end of the Egyptian and the beginning of the Ottoman counter-Crusades against Rhodes, a number of developments took place which radically changed the course of history in the Levant. On 29 May 1453, Constantinople fell to Mohammed the Conqueror and the Byzantine city became the Ottoman capital. Rhodes was now menaced as never before and for the next seventy years it remained the sole eastern bulwark of Christianity.

Mohammed lost no time in demanding tribute from the Holy Religion and such pressures had long been put on Rhodes. Failing in his attempts to persuade the Knights to purchase immunity from attack by the payment of an annual levy, a powerful expeditionary force led by Misac Pasha was despatched to Rhodes and appeared off the island on 23 May 1480. Two hundred ships anchored under the hill of Monte Smith and with the landing of cavalry, janissaries and artillery, the first great siege of Rhodes commenced.

The initial assault took place around the fortress of St Nicholas, which was the key to the city's defences from the sea. It was followed by an assault on the section of walls adjacent to the Jewish quarter. This was a vulnerable part of the total defences and the Knights were forced to demolish dwellings adjacent to the wall, thereby creating a second line of defence, separated from the original by a moat. Further assaults were again directed against the fort of St Nicholas and other sections of the wall. The Knights proved too stubborn for the Turkish onslaught and on 3 August, the siege was lifted. It is reported that the Turks left behind some 15,000 casualties. To celebrate their victory the Knights built a large church dedicated to the Virgin Mary—'Our Lady of the Victory'.

THE SIEGE OF SULEIMAN

The Moslem conquest of most of the Aegean islands by Bayazid II in 1502 followed on that of the Peloponnesus (1499), but Rhodes found that it was able to maintain its stand provided that the major Moslem powers in Egypt and Western Asia could be kept apart or at war. In 1516, however, the Battle of Marj Dabiq, near Aleppo, was fought between Selim I (1512–20) of Turkey and the Mamluk Sultan Qansuh al-Chauri (1500–16) of Egypt and the result drastically changed Rhodes' position. The Egyptian sultan fell in the field and Syria was annexed to Turkey. Then, in 1517, the Battle of al-Raydaniya, north-east of Cairo, sealed the fate of Egypt itself. The triumph of the Ottomans in both these decisive battles was due not merely to their numerical and tactical superiority, but also to their use of new artillery and gunpowder, unknown to the Egyptian soldier. The results were clear—the Levant was transformed into one huge Ottoman domain.

The fall of Rhodes was indeed only delayed until Selim I had consolidated the Moslem dominions in the Near East. It was obvious that a renewed attempt on the eastern outpost of Christianity would be made, lying as it did across the main sea route from Constantinople to Alexandria. Two years after his succession, Sultan Suleiman II (the Magnificent) mounted a siege on Rhodes which lasted from 28 June to 22 December

1522. Three hundred ships and over 100,000 men are said to have made up the Ottoman force and although these figures may be suspect, there is no doubt that the besiegers possessed an overwhelming majority. The Knights, it is estimated, mustered 650, with the addition of 6,000 Rhodians trained for war, 400 Cretans, 200 Genoese and 50 Venetians.

The island put up tremendous resistance in a siege which lasted for 177 days. The enemy forces with their cannons took up initial positions on Monte Smith and the army under the direction of generals, or pashas, surrounded the landward defences. The manoeuvres were in many ways a repetition of those of the 1480 siege. The first assault was conducted against the north-western (Germanic) walls and the St Nicholas fortress. Repeated charges by the Turks were repulsed as were the attempts to tunnel under the walls. On 4 September the Turks succeeded in capturing part of the Post of England, only to be regained by the Knights at a cost, it is reported, of 2,000 enemy casualties. Another attempt a few days later met with a similar fate, and on 13 September the Turks were also driven back from the Post of Italy. Suleiman, impatient with the repeated failures of his troops, conducted a general assault against the Post of Aragon on 24 September, but following a loss of 15,000 men, a retreat was ordered. Blame for the failure was levelled against General Mustapha Pasha who was replaced by Ahmed Pasha as the new Chief of Staff.

Suleiman, greatly discouraged by his losses, spoke of lifting the siege and admitting defeat. His victory came through the treachery of one of the Knights, Andrea d'Amaral, the titular head of the Tongue of Castile. The Sultan was informed that the Rhodian forces had greatly diminished, that the long-expected help from Europe was not forthcoming and that, within the city, food and ammunitions were near exhaustion. The siege continued and on 22 December a final assault on the Post of Aragon took the city by sheer weight of numbers. Grand Master Villiers de l'Isle Adam surrendered the city and island

Page 89 (*above*) The temple of Athena on the acropolis of Lindos; (*below*) a Doric
fountain of the fourth century BC at Ialysos

Page 90 (above) The reconstructed Palace of the Grand Masters, Rhodes; (below) the monumental structure of the Marine Gate links the medieval town with the Commercial Harbour

but negotiated terms under which the Knights and the general population were guaranteed their lives.

The Order was allowed a respite of twelve days to leave the island and all Rhodians wishing to follow them into exile were free to do so, taking with them any possessions they could carry. Suleiman also pledged the safety of those wishing to remain and further decreed that the city was to be exempt from taxation for a period of five years.

Escorted by 4,000 inhabitants who preferred exile to Ottoman rule the Knights left Rhodes on 1 January 1523. Their departure put an end to the sporadic proposals for further Crusades as the capture of the island now left the whole Aegean under Turkish sovereignty. Suleiman took the necessary measures to ensure its retention, leaving a garrison of 1,800 janissaries with a score of galleys and he ordered the reconstruction of the city's damaged defences. 'Nothing in the world was ever so well lost as was Rhodes,' remarked Emperor Charles V of Spain, on hearing the story of the great siege of 1522. The Knights withdrew initially to Viterbo and Civitavecchia, but by 1530 they had established themselves in Malta, under a grant of Charles V.

F

5   TURK AND ITALIAN

IT would be unfair to perpetuate the view of the Turkish
period on Rhodes as one of unmitigated disaster. Although
the records of the 390 years of occupation (1522–1912) are
scanty and there is little in print beyond the descriptions of
occasional travellers and various references in histories of
Greece, Turkey and the Levant, the island was again to reap
certain advantages from its position and its natural resources
maintained a degree of prosperity.

More detailed accounts of Rhodes stem from visitors to the
island during the nineteenth century, a time when the Ottoman
Empire was rapidly disintegrating and Turkish administration,
inefficient and corrupt, continued steadily to decline. This
characteristic Turkish indolence and inertia is blamed for the
fall in prestige of Rhodes and for the apathy and sluttishness
that persisted on a grand scale. 'Rhodes,' writes Newton in
1865, 'is a place which has long wasted away with that atrophy
which is consuming the Ottoman Empire. The town is far too
large for its inhabitants who are huddled away in holes and
corners. About a year ago an earthquake threw down one of
the fine old towers. Its ruins fell in one of the principal streets,
blocking it up. Not a stone has been touched by the Turks, and
the ruins may perhaps lie there till another earthquake shakes
them up again.'

The Turkish unconcern, which by the nineteenth century had
produced effects of a negative, wasting kind, did not apply to
Rhodes during the earlier years of Turkish rule. The island,
however, was not fortunate to receive the privileges which

Suleiman accorded to other Dodecanese islands. Through a certain amount of diplomatic skill, Simi, Kalymnos and other islands succeeded in obtaining a firman from Suleiman, guaranteeing them autonomy under Turkish sovereignty and the right to retain armed fortresses. These concessions were merely a continuation of the conditions which operated in ancient times and which were respected by the Romans, the Byzantines and the Knights. The firman of Suleiman was further confirmed by a series of successive sultans and as a result of the liberal terms the group became known as the 'privileged islands'. The only limit to freedom was the island tribute, the *maktou*, which was not excessive and was normally spent on local Moslem institutions.

The Turks had taken Rhodes and Kos by force and consequently they were administered along the lines of other conquered provinces with a resident governor and a garrison. The distinction between Greek and Turk was again embodied in the payment of the *maktou* or capitulation tax, collected once a year by a government functionary. There is evidence that the Rhodians suffered from the unfair way in which the tribute was administered. The right of collection was sold by the government to the highest bidder who in turn often sold it at a profit to others. The fleecing of peasants, merchants and tradesmen was common and further exactions by provincial governors were often ruinous to the individual. Another measure, common to all Ottoman territories, was the segregation of Moslem and non-Moslem subjects and any real contact between Turk and Greek was rigidly suppressed. In Rhodes the Greeks were excluded from the old city at night and were forced to develop new settlements outside the walls. A cannon or bell proclaimed the closing of the gates and only Turks and Jews were authorised to remain, and live, within the fortified city.

RHODES

ECONOMIC AND CULTURAL AUTONOMY

In spite of the above measures, the fact remains that Rhodes was allowed considerable latitude under its Turkish conquerors and the island was able to maintain many of the benefits of the past. With few exceptions the Turks did not actively participate in the economic development of the island. Attachment to the Turkish Empire proved beneficial to the Rhodians and they quickly used the natural advantages of their geographical position. The Turks with military insolence and peasant ignorance, regarded all trade and commerce as undignified and allowed the Rhodians to trade freely with other parts of the empire and with Europe. This succeeded in returning some of the transit cargo which had formerly made the port of Rhodes prosperous, and, prior to steam replacing sail, it became an important refurbishing base for shipping between Levantine ports and Greece. The Lindians, too, with their tradition in seafaring, plied the trade routes from Rhodes to mainland Greece, Constantinople and Egypt. On the local level, agricultural products such as fruits, oil, hides, olives and wine were exchanged for Turkish sugar, wheat, rice and animal produce. Vouros estimates that during the Turkish period about 10 per cent of the island's working population was engaged in shipping and trade.

The significance of commerce fostered shipbuilding which utilised local timber supplies. The principal types of ships built were naval vessels for the Porte and sponge-fishing vessels for the islanders of Kalymnos, Simi and Chalki. The industry prospered until the nineteenth century when the local timber resources were depleted. Many Rhodians emigrated to the shipyards of Greece and Turkey for there was little restriction on population movement. The Turkish mainland, in particular, provided the islanders with alternative employment opportunities and it was not difficult for Rhodian masons, carpenters,

94

shipbuilders and traders to find work in the cities of Constantinople and Smyrna or in centres in Egypt and the Levant. Other Rhodian industries were textiles and ceramics. They were handicraft and cottage industries and utilised both local and imported raw materials. The products found ready markets in Turkey and Europe where they circulated under the name 'Turkish' ware.

Rhodes also gained other advantages under the Ottoman regime. The genius of the Turks was for conquest rather than administration and as far as possible they employed their conquered subjects to run the machinery of the empire. The subject peoples were classified according to their religion— church and state were regarded as virtually synonymous. Under this *millet* system the Greek community was granted almost complete cultural autonomy within the framework of its church. The Rhodians were permitted to regulate their own finances, to appoint their own officials, and the Turks made no attempt at wholesale conversion of the Greeks to Islam. It is true that all Latin churches were converted into mosques and the Latin bishop was sent into exile with the Knights, but the majority of the Orthodox churches survived and in 1524 there is reference to a Greek Metropolitan Bishop. It may be that Suleiman regarded his lenient terms as applying only to the Greeks, but since most of the Latin settlers had left Rhodes with the Order, there was little need for Latin churches. The Turkish regime, therefore, was for the most part a tolerant one and Voltaire's comment that the Greek clergy preferred the turban of a Turkish priest to the red hat of a Roman cardinal is admirably illustrated by the fate of the Church of Rhodes under Turkish and, subsequently, Italian rule. The deliberate policy of the Turks of isolating themselves from the Greeks ensured the endurance of Greek characteristics and this must be regarded as the strongest factor in the survival of the Greek way of life.

THE ORIENTAL SCENE

The main impact of the Turkish regime was felt (and, today, is visually represented) in Rhodes city and its immediate surroundings, where the Turks were mainly concentrated. The ratio of Turks to Greeks varied throughout the period of occupation from one in five to one in twenty. A seventeenth-century estimate gave the population as 15,000 Greeks, 1,200 Turks and 200 Jews. A record for the eighteenth century quotes the figures as being 18,000, 3,000 and 500 respectively. Around 1850, the Countess Dora d'Istria visited the island and spoke of 6,000 Turks residing in the Castello (Collachium) quarter of the city and 20,000 Greeks occupying the suburbs and villages.

Although it is a common criticism that 'the Turk built nothing', the old town of Rhodes during the nineteenth century had a distinctive, if superficial and temporary, oriental air. A number of descriptions and engravings furnish information on its form and character. It was still contained within the medieval fortifications and its subdivisions corresponded to the old Collachium and Bourg. An irregular maze of narrow streets and alleyways, punctuated by mosques, minarets, fountains and shaded courtyards provided the Turkish fabric and it appears that even the Street of the Knights had assumed an oriental appearance with jutting wooden balconies precariously attached to the medieval facades. Visitors were horrified to see the uses the Turks had made of the medieval buildings and Thakeray (in *Notes of a Journey from Cornhill to Grand Cairo*) was moved to comment that 'now the famous house is let to a shabby merchant'. The inns and hospital were used as dwellings and barracks, the Palace of the Grand Master became a prison and its chapel a cattle shed. The Commercial Courts served as both cattle shed and mosque.

Largely because of the exclusion of the Greeks, sections of the town were untenanted, but scattered throughout it were

96

numerous mosques and there was also a Jewish quarter with several synagogues. Rhodes also contained three Mohammedan colleges, Turkish schools and a library. The mosques, most of which are now in a state of decay, belonged to two classes— those built specifically as mosques and those that were converted from Christian churches, some having subsequently been re-consecrated for Orthodox purposes. Belonging to the former group is the Mosque of Suleiman, erected soon after 1522 in honour of the conqueror of Rhodes. The mosque was rebuilt in the early years of the nineteenth century and remains in use. Other mosques adding to the oriental character of the old town include Hamza Bey, Chadreven, Sultan Mustafa, Retjep Pasha, Ibrahim Pasha and the Agha Mosque, the latter being the place of worship of the Turkish garrison commander. The mosques of Suleiman, Ibrahim Pasha, and Redjeb Pasha, together with three or four others, are all small buildings with a square interior, a cupola supported by pendentives and a single minaret. They are bordered by a portico and are preceded by the customary court with tree, usually a palm, and fountain. Rhodes also possessed a number of hammams or public baths and that of Sultan Mustafa is still used.

To the west and south of the medieval walls were two ceme-teries. The Turkish one extended from the Amboise Gate to the Koskinou Gate and the Jewish one, lying immediately outside the Jewish quarter, was bounded by the Koskinou Gate and Acandia Bay. They were bordered by extensive gardens and to the south were the expanding Greek suburbs of St Anargyrous, St Anastasia and St George. In the north-west was the suburb of Neo Chorio or Neo Maras, which by the nineteenth century contained the British and French vice-consulates and the Roman Catholic church. It became the new Frankish quarter of Rhodes and although containing Greeks, a large proportion of the population professed the Latin faith. Bordering the port of Mandraki was the arsenal and the Pasha's palace, harem and gardens. Further north, and adjacent to the lazaretto or

97

warehouse, was the mosque of Mourad-Reis and the Mufti's residence.

Throughout the Turkish period, as today, the economy of Rhodes was basically agrarian. In the countryside the Turkish influence was mainly felt through the workings of the Moslem law of land ownership and inheritance, common to the Turkish mainland. The majority of peasants farmed their lands as tenants of either the state, on *emiri* or domain land, or of religious institutions on *vakouf* land. Five-tenths of the cultivated acreage belonged to the *emiri* category and two-tenths to the *vakouf* category. *Emiri* was officially the property of the sultan or Porte and could be reclaimed if it remained uncultivated for a period of ten years. A portion of this land was assigned to the offices controlled by the viziers.

The agricultural land was owned by absentee-landlords whose large estates made up what was called the *beylik* or home farm. The economic and social status of the tenants depended on the quality of the farm and also on the wealth and character of the landlord. The conditions of tenancy varied considerably but in all cases the landlord provided the farmer with a stable, donkey or mule, seed and a barn. In return the tenant either paid a fixed rent (usually about two bushels of wheat per acre) or divided the crop equally with the landowner. In addition to the above categories the Greek peasantry were permitted to hold land that technically was their own. This *mulk* land and its usufructuary rights passed automatically to their heirs, provided the lands were not neglected and the taxes regularly paid. Three-tenths of the cultivated area belonged to the *mulk* category as well as much urban property.

The categories of land, though theoretically sound, were cumbersome and confused in their application, but they caused relatively little hardship to the peasant. It was possible, however, for landowners to exploit their tenant labour, and this exploitation, together with the small size of holdings which averaged not more than three acres, led to extensive emigration to Asia Minor where agricultural land was cheap. The acquisition of land in the vicinity of cities such as Constantinople and Smyrna was common. It was only during the nineteenth century, however, that the lot of the Rhodian peasant became one of abject poverty and misery. This was the result of excessive taxation introduced by the Turks in an oppressive policy levelled against the islanders.

DECLINE AND OPPRESSION

Towards the end of the eighteenth century the relative economic importance of Rhodes under the Turkish regime began to decline. The exhaustion of timber supplies for shipbuilding and the decline in cottage handicrafts when factory-made textile goods became easily available resulted in the displacement of workers and widespread emigration. The development of steamship navigation decreased the role of the island as a port of call in the eastern Mediterranean and the construction of a large warehouse failed to attract any volume of shipping. The island also suffered as the political situation in Western Europe and the Balkans became less and less favourable to the Ottoman Empire and the indifferent Turkish rule was quickly replaced by one that was harsh and marked by excessive taxation and terrorism.

During the Greek national revolution against the Turks in the early decades of the nineteenth century, Rhodes was unable to participate openly in the general uprising. Many islanders, however, took up arms under the leadership of Greek chiefs on the mainland and Rhodes was able to send delegates to the first Greek National Conference at Nauplion in the Peloponnesus. The Turks, fearing revolution, imposed ruthless controls on every aspect of Rhodian life and nineteenth-century commentaries speak of slaughter, misery and squalor. Outright suppres-

99

sion began in 1866 when the Turks initiated a campaign for the forceful integration of Rhodes and the Dodecanese into the Ottoman way of life. By 1871 Turkish tribunals had replaced the local Greek courts and by 1874 Turkish control of harbours and customs was complete. Under the Young Turks' regime heavy taxation methods were introduced and the 'ancient privileges' entirely rescinded. Turkish was decreed to be the official language, compulsory military subscription was introduced and religious liberties abrogated. Further measures included making the possession of arms an act punishable by death and the setting up of an extensive network of spies. Massacres without cause ostensibly served as examples of what would happen if Rhodes joined the Greek rebellion.

In the Balkan War of 1912, Greece, Serbia, Montenegro and Bulgaria joined hands against Turkey for the final settlement of their irredentist claims, and the Greek fleet succeeded in liberating the northern Aegean islands of Lesbos, Chios, Samos and Ikaria. The liberation of Rhodes and the Dodecanese seemed imminent. Italy, however, was independently at war with Turkey and although this event precipitated the expulsion of the Turks from the European provinces, it also prohibited the union of the Dodecanese with Greece for another thirty-five years.

The Italian-Turkish War (the Libyan War) of 1911–12 formed part of Italy's active colonial expansion in North Africa. It was fought on the pretext that the Turks had stirred up trouble against Italy and resisted Italian economic penetration in North Africa. Within a month of September 1911 the Turkish-controlled coastal towns of Tripolitania and Cyrenaica had fallen, but there was no decisive victory as the Arab populations of the desert interior proved more difficult to subjugate than the Turkish troops. From Libya the war spread to the Dodecanese and Asia Minor and early in 1912 an Italian expeditionary force assembled at Astypalaea and occupied most of the islands without resistance. On Rhodes, the Turkish garrison withdrew to Psithnos where on 17 May a fierce and decisive battle was fought. The Turks officially signed their surrender and the Italian occupation of the Dodecanese began.

THE ITALIANS

The Italians announced that they had not come as conquerors and that their stay in the Dodecanese would be only temporary. Not surprisingly the Rhodians gave them an enthusiastic welcome, looking upon them as their liberators from Turkish yoke. Italy in return gave the islanders assurances of 'the greatest possible proofs of goodwill', of 'the respect of your religion, your customs and your tradition', and of 'complete autonomy in the future' after a 'provisional occupation'. There was no reason for the Rhodians to believe that the Italian statements were idle promises and the Italian Premier, Giolitti, repudiated the notion of 'annexing territories of Greek nationality'. It was explained that the islands were occupied to ensure that Turkey would fulfil the terms of the peace settlement in North Africa.

In June 1912, a congress of Dodecanese island delegates met in Patmos and voted for the establishment of a free Aegean state whose first duty would be to give effect to the permanent national wish of all Greeks to be incorporated into the Kingdom of Greece. The Treaty of Lausanne (October 1912), however, which ended the first Balkan War, provided for the return of the Dodecanese to Turkey as soon as the Turkish evacuation of the Libyan provinces of Cyrenaica and Tripolitania was completed. Greek confidence in the Allies was further embittered when Turkey entered the 1914–18 war and, consequently, the Treaty of London (April 1915) laid down that 'Italy shall be acknowledged as possessing total sovereignty over the Dodecanese Islands it occupies at present'. This was a principle accepted by both France and Britain. The Italians argued that on the resumption of hostilities the Treaty of Lausanne lapsed, and that their occupation of the islands must be treated as conquest.

As part of the peace settlements of 1919–23, the Greek Prime Minister, Venizelos, with the help of Britain, obtained from Italy an agreement to assign the Dodecanese to Greece. This was confirmed in 1920 by the Treaty of Sèvres. The important exception was Rhodes which was to be given local autonomy in which to exercise an option by plebiscite under the League of Nations. The Tittoni-Venizelos accord was repudiated by Italy in 1922, the Treaty of Sèvres being still unratified, and the second Treaty of Lausanne (1924) again confirmed Italy in full possession of the Dodecanese. Britain continued to back the Greek claim for the islands and urged Italy to honour its earlier agreement.

The reluctance of Italy to cede the islands must be viewed in the light of the country's long desire for expansion in the eastern Mediterranean. Acquisition of the Dodecanese was an important first step before Italian penetration of Asia Minor could be contemplated. With the rise of Mussolini and Fascism, Italian policy was transformed into renascent Roman autocracy and Rhodes, in particular, experienced a period of oppression and tyranny much more painful and harrowing than anything suffered under the Turks. Such are the vagaries of international politics that in 1928 a pact of friendship was concluded between Greece and Italy. Mussolini assured Venizelos that Italy would not follow a policy of denationalisation in the Dodecanese and this promise was repeated on several occasions. In point of fact the Italians took active measures to eradicate Greek culture from the islands and to stifle any hopes of union with Greece. In 1937, the new governor, de Vecchi, announced that he had come 'to bring Fascist life and the Fascist spirit to the islands'.

THE ITALIAN IMPACT

The first infringement of freedom came with interference in local government. This culminated in March 1937, when the municipal council of the City of Rhodes, which the Turks never molested, was dissolved, together with other municipalities. The Orthodox Church was also suppressed and religious rites were interfered with. In education the municipal and endowed schools were brought under the Italian educational authority and teaching was assimilated to Italian state schools. Many schools and colleges were closed and their buildings used as military offices by Fascist organisations. Italian became the compulsory language of education and children were ordered to speak it, even out of school. Italian teachers replaced Greek and the latter were barred from entering the island.

The Italian policy was also active in breaking up the traditional land-tenure system and in deranging the social structure of the Greek peasantry. Forced sales of land at arbitrary low prices ruined many farmers and separated them from inherited properties. Land expropriated under the pretext of afforestation or military use was often subsequently given to Italian immigrants. Rigid control was also enforced over intercourse with Greece, Turkey, and even between islands within the Dodecanese.

Brutal as the Italian policy was to the national integrity of the Rhodians, in a material sense the island benefited, and still benefits today, from the works of their past rulers. Rhodes was administered with scientific skill and lavish expenditure, though much was undoubtedly done as propaganda and to impress the local population. Roads were built, villas and garden suburbs laid out and a large number of pretentious public buildings erected. The Italians also laid down the groundwork of the present flourishing tourist industry and pointed

103

the way towards a more intensive and productive use of the land. Irrigation and reclamation projects were common.

The academic interests of the Italians were directed, primarily, to archaeology and they excavated many classical and Hellenistic sites and restored or rebuilt a number of historical monuments. The much criticised restoration of the Palace of the Grand Master was their biggest project. The exterior of the palace is, as far as possible, a reconstruction of the fourteenth-century building and was completed before the last war. The interior was designed for modern occupation, the intention being to use it as a summer residence for Victor Emmanuel III and Mussolini. A special throne was brought from Italy and electricity, central heating, lifts and other comforts were installed. On completion, and to celebrate the new imperial pretentions of Fascism, Mussolini ordered an inscription to be placed at the entrance to the palace. In large gold capitals can be read the words: 'During the reign of his majesty Victor Emmanuel III, King of Italy and Albania and Emperor of Ethiopia, with Benito Mussolini, the Duke of Fascism, at the head of government and Cesare Maria de Vecchi, Count of Val Cismon, the governor of the Italian islands of the Aegean, this ancient fortress, built by the Knights of St John on the unprofaned Roman defence was reconstructed and restored, giving back strength and splendour to its new role as the seat of government of the city of fortitude, defender of western civilisation under the rule and religion of Rome. (The year of our Lord, 1940, eighteenth year of the Fascist era.)'

Ironically the preparations were barely complete when Italy was plunged into World War II and was forced to relinquish its colonial empires in Africa and the Aegean. The thirty-three years occupation of Rhodes had cost the Italians much in terms of men, money and emotional commitment.

WAR AND LIBERATION

The value of Rhodes as a vital strategic Mediterranean base again became apparent during World War II. Churchill regarded the island as the key to wartime strategy in the Aegean area. With the fall of Mussolini and the surrender of Italy the Allies had the opportunity of gaining Rhodes and the Dodecanese at very little cost and effort. Rhodes possessed good air and naval bases from which the Allies could operate in defence of the Aegean and the eastern Mediterranean and there was also the important naval base of Leros and an air base on Kos. It was realised that the British air forces in Egypt and Cyrenaica would be able to defend Alexandria, Cairo and Suez just as efficiently, or even better, if detachments moved forward to Rhodes. Conversely it was feared that if the Luftwaffe commenced operations from the Dodecanese the whole Mediterranean coast from Haifa to Apollonia in Cyrenaica would be within range of enemy bombers.

Hitler's appreciation of the situation agreed with Churchill's for Allied possession of Rhodes would have opened up the Aegean northwards as far as Izmir, thereby creating more favourable conditions for a general assault on Crete where the Germans were in strength. Churchill also saw that possession of the Dodecanese would be an added inducement for Turkey to enter the war on the side of the Allies. Britain needed use of the Turkish air bases to maintain a tighter grip on the eastern Mediterranean.

In September 1943, the Dodecanese were occupied by two Italian divisions and one German division. On Rhodes Italian morale was low but the Greek population was excited by their confidence that the Allies would liberate the islands. Plans and preparations for an assault on the Dodecanese had been perfected in the Middle East Command and they were kept under constant review in Cairo. Churchill called on Roosevelt and

Eisenhower for aid in the assault on Rhodes and stressed the danger of allowing the Germans time to consolidate there. The Americans were planning the Salerno landing and were not prepared to release ships and planes. The British plans were further frustrated by the subsequent decision by the Combined Chiefs of Staff in Quebec to send five out of eight landing ships, held temporarily in the Middle East, to the Indian Ocean. It is now known that Roosevelt suspected British intentions in Greece and was unconvinced by Churchill's argument that control of the Dodecanese was 'a prize beyond compare'.

On the announcement of the Italian surrender a small party of British troops landed on Rhodes. Their objective was to contact the Italians and to persuade them to take the German garrison, pending the arrival by sea of Allied support. The Italians finally agreed but the Germans were thoroughly prepared and a short battle left them in complete control of the island. The Germans expected a general assault on their south-eastern flank and the heads of both the army and navy favoured the evacuation of the Aegean, but Hitler overruled. The British succeeded in taking Kos, Samos and Leros and each had a battalion of troops, and a company was established on Kastellorizo. These positions were precarious and untenable as long as the Germans held Rhodes and within three days of the British arrival on Kos heavy air bombardment prepared the way for the major counter-attack on 3 October. The other islands received similar treatment and when Leros fell on 16 November the Dodecanese were again under enemy control. It is reported that during these operations the British army losses were 4,800 men and the Royal Air Force lost 115 aircraft. It is estimated that the Germans lost 4,000 men and 21,000 tons of shipping. The British and Greek naval losses in the Aegean had also been severe, amounting to 6 destroyers, 2 submarines and 10 coastal craft lost, and 4 cruisers and 4 destroyers damaged. These losses serve to illustrate the great

Page 107 (*right*) The Street of the Knights preserves the medieval atmosphere of the Collachium quarter; (*below*) Socrates Street, the main bazaar of the old Turkish town, is dominated by the Mosque of Suleiman, rebuilt at the beginning of the nineteenth century

Page 108 (*left*) Mosques and minarets punctuate the town-scape of the now largely ruined Turkish quarter; (*below*) a fountain belonging to the Turkish period

value both sides placed on the possession of the Dodecanese.

It is now known that the details and episodes involving Rhodes and the Aegean islands constituted the most acute differences Churchill had with Eisenhower during the whole war campaigns. Little was gained from the British operations and German control of the Aegean remained for some considerable time. Furthermore, Turkish neutrality continued intact until the last months of the war. Roughly a year later the Germans were forced to evacuate Greece as a result of a series of events elsewhere and an almost bloodless takeover by the Allies followed in October 1944. German troops, however, remained on Crete, Rhodes and other islands, and only with the surrender of Germany were they liberated by Greek and British forces.

The end of the war again brought to light the unsolved question of the Dodecanese and Britain, confirming Roosevelt's earlier suspicions, made a bold move to retain the islands. Following a bitter diplomatic exchange in June 1946, the Dodecanese were granted union with Greece and in May 1947 the British military command was turned over to Vice-Admiral Pericles Ioannides of the Greek navy. The official union was achieved in March 1948 when Paul I, King of Hellenes, arrived in Rhodes.

Both the Italian and German occupations survive as bitter memories to the Rhodians, but it is interesting to note that they have not troubled to remove Mussolini's magniloquent inscription from the entrance to the Palace of the Grand Master. Instead, adjacent to the Italian notice is a Greek statement accompanied by a clumsy English translation. It reads: 'Reigning Paul on the twenty-ninth of June, nineteen hundred and forty-seven, by decision of the Military Governor of the Dodecanese, Vice-Admiral Pericles Ioannides, this rebuilt palace of the Great Magister of the Knights has been declared an historical monument to be preserved, thus rendered to the history of the unconquered Dodecanese people, who have

G

maintained undiminished, during all foreign occupations, the idea of freedom, inexhaustible fountain of the eternal Greek civilisation.'

6   THE ISLANDERS AS GREEKS

IN spite of a long history of disruptive forces, the contemporary Rhodian population is essentially Greek in its culture and general way of life. Customs and traditions handed down through centuries of invasion and occupation continue to form the basis of everyday life, and all foreign elements, whether medieval or modern in origin, have been assimilated to the traditional thought and ethos of the people. Commentators on modern Rhodes have remarked on the continuity of the island's culture and the manner in which it has preserved certain standards and aspirations through many political changes. The survival of ethnic character, national identity, language and religion can be related, as was stated in Chapter 1, to the Rhodians' acute awareness of, and intense pride in, their Greekness. This was most apparent during the nineteenth century when Rhodes lay outside the confines of the emerging independent Greek state. The islanders contrived to maintain a corporate existence and consciousness of ethnic and cultural unity with Greece was sustained chiefly through the Orthodox Church and the Greek language. During the early decades of this century Greek culture received its most powerful blows when the Italian administration did everything in its power to suppress the Greek way of life. The major pivots of Hellenism, the church and the Greek language, were brutally attacked as were other traditional institutions such as local self-government and the ownership and occupancy of land. The Italian policies were unsuccessful in breaking the cultural bond between the island and Greece: if anything they served to strengthen local patriotism and self-determination. For these reasons, many authors have agreed that cultural domination over the island cannot be anything but a rule of force.

THE ORTHODOX CHURCH

The island's cultural link with the past is most apparent in its religious beliefs and practices. From the time St Paul, on his way to Rome, is said to have landed at the small bay that bears his name in Lindos, the church has been the consolation and inspiration of the Rhodian people. Under the Turks the church with its annual cycle of rite and worship became the medium of preserving and handing on from generation to generation all that was vital to Greek life and cultural survival. This solid attachment to Orthodoxy remains, and the contemporary church is a potent factor in Rhodian life.

The Church of Rhodes and the Dodecanese is an autonomous institution and is not controlled by the church of the Greek mainland. It owes its allegiance directly to the Oecumenical Patriarch of Constantinople, a fact which in itself stresses the continuity of the church which has remained faithful to the roots and sources of earliest Christianity. The church is headed by the Metropolitan Bishop of Rhodes and included within the local diocese are the islands of Tilos, Nisyros, Chalki and Simi. Over 90 per cent of the island's population are nominally members of the Orthodox Church which to the Rhodian is virtually a symbol or badge of Greek nationalism. The chief religious minorities are Moslem and Jewish groups, headed by a Mufti and Rabbi, respectively, and a number of Roman Catholics and Protestants.

The Italians made persistent efforts to undermine the cultural and political powers of the bishop and the church on the pretext that ministers of religion in Italian territory should not be dependent on outside ecclesiastical authority. The real reasons went deeper for the Greek Church has always been closely associated with the political and national life of its people and during periods of occupation it was the clergy who helped to keep the Greeks' identity and aspirations alive. In 1921 the Metropolitan Bishop of Rhodes was expelled after pressure had been put on him to sever his connections with Constantinople. Constitutionally this was not in his power. A further move to suppress the influence of the church came in 1930 when the mixed religious and lay courts were closed. The Italians also ruled that the appointment of bishops and priests was to be conditional on government approval. On the local level there was interference with Orthodox ritual, including the rites for marriages and burials, and church festivals and pilgrimages were prohibited. These measures, together with the intensive Catholic propaganda, were deeply resented by the Rhodians who saw them as a complete reversal of the Ottoman policy which had left the church largely unmolested.

The refinements of Greek Orthodox practice are complex, but its basic doctrines are largely those of the western Trinitarian churches. Some beliefs and the basic form of worship loosely parallel Roman Catholicism, though Orthodoxy refuses to recognise the primacy of the Pope and is not autocratic in the Catholic style. Religion tends to be ritualised and impersonal and it incorporates much of local origin. The church hierarchy has a status analogous to the civil service or the military and the Metropolitan Bishop of Rhodes has the 'rank' of a general and is saluted by the military when he carries out his official duties. The bishops and other high officers are celibate and are recruited from monastic institutions.

On the local level the priest, or *papas*, is the most influential, and frequently, the best-educated person in rural communities. He is appointed by the bishop and is allowed to marry, although this prevents him from rising higher in the church hierarchy or entering a monastery. Normally, the priest lives exactly as the ordinary villager and usually has either land, or a business, to supplement his small stipend of which about one-quarter comes from the parish. Virtually no enterprise is undertaken without priestly blessing and he is consulted whenever difficulties arise either in the home or in the parish at large.

The Rhodian landscape is dominated by the material manifestations of Orthodoxy. All villages have at least one domed, red-roofed, Byzantine-styled church, generally complete with an ornate bell-tower. The church is the centre of the local community and is usually closely associated with the village school. Each church is dedicated to the local saint of the district and its lavish decoration and pretentiousness contrasts with the humbler buildings of rural communities. Many Rhodian churches date back to Byzantine foundations, but even newer buildings slavishly follow the traditional architectural form with arch, circle, dome and cross and whose impression of architectural simplicity is deceptive. Churches and wayside shrines also appear as isolated features of the landscape, particularly on hill-tops or on coastal promontories. Many are small and are used only on one day of the year to commemorate a particular saint or the name-day of the founder.

The internal arrangement of churches follows a standard pattern. A screen of icons (the *iconostasis*) divides the sanctuary from the nave where the congregation stands throughout the service. Attached to various icons are small metal tags (*tamata* or *taximata*)—simulacra moulded in the image of the part of a body, an animal or a person the petitioner wants cured or protected. Most churches have at least one miraculous icon as well as other venerated relics.

Monasticism plays an important part in Greek Orthodoxy and a large number of monasteries exist on Rhodes with interesting architecture, frescoes, histories and legends. The hospitality they offer to travellers may be the only accommodation available in some remoter areas. The term *monastiri*, however, is often applied to lonely chapels and recalls the former use of these places by hermits.

THE GREEK LANGUAGE

Language has been the other major pillar in the cultural survival of the Rhodian population. The Rhodian speaks a dialect of modern Greek which is a powerful determinant of nationalism. Modern Greek constitutes the present stage in the natural development of the language from classical Greek, through *koine* or New Testament Greek, and Byzantine or medieval Greek, to the present day. Like all languages it has undergone various changes in pronunciation, grammar and vocabulary throughout its historical course, but the modern tongue has preserved a remarkable number of qualities of the original stock and has maintained a unity unparalleled by any other European language. It is often pointed out that the oldest literature in the language, the Homeric poems, is far more intelligible to the modern Greek than Chaucer is to English speakers.

The fact remains, however, that modern Greek is a language in transition and one that is experimental in form and open to new usages and influences. A striking feature of the modern language is the instability of spelling, found even among the commonest words. Many of these differences arise from the distinction between the 'demotic' and 'puristic' forms of speech. Colloquial Greek is a mixture of both, with demotic predominating. The puristic form, *katharevousa*, is more formal in style and is used mainly in writing official documents, some textbooks and partly in newspapers, the latter employing a mixed speech known as *kathomiloumeni*. The struggle between the various forms continues and to understand this confusion it is necessary to trace briefly the historical development of Greek.

The ancient language knew a number of dialects and although they stemmed from a combination of geographical isolation and variation in customs and political organisation, they rarely showed any tendency to develop into separate tongues. The classical dialects such as Ionian, Dorian and Aeolian had disappeared by the Hellenistic period. As a result of Alexander's conquests, Greek culture attained a dominating commercial and intellectual influence in the eastern Mediterranean and the Middle East and a more standardised speech developed as a general instrument of communication. In the first century BC *koine* (common Greek), which rested heavily on the Ionian-Attic dialect, became the language current in Hellenised regions.

The Romans made little attempt to displace *koine*, though a number of Latin words and idioms were incorporated into Greek. Over the centuries, through the rise and fall of the Byzantine Empire, a gap developed between the language of the masses and the more refined language of the lettered and the church. The vulgar tongue absorbed foreign words and idioms and each region developed its own dialect. A northern group of dialects extended from Epirus to Thrace and Lesbos; a south-western group covered the Ionian Islands, the Peloponnesus, Crete and the Cyclades; an eastern group embraced the whole of Asia Minor and the islands of the Asiatic seaboard from Chios to Cyprus. The variations in speech had reached their widest span by the eighteenth century and with the establishment of Greek independence in the nineteenth century a movement to impose a unified and purified language gained the support of many educated classes. The artificial language, *katharevousa*, stemmed basically from the cultural revival in the Ionian Islands and it was adopted as the official state language after liberation.

Katharevousa was never thoroughly understood on the lower social levels and towards the end of the nineteenth century a new 'school' arose, consisting mainly of poets and writers, who upheld the claims of the popular language. The biggest reaction came in the 1880s when the controversy over the language question flared up in a violent form as a result of the publication of a polemical work, *My Journey*, by John Psycharis.

Written in demotic, he advocated the abolition of *katharevousa* and the adoption of the popular tongue as the language of the state, scholarship and literature. His theories were fiercely opposed on all levels, but they were welcomed by many men of letters. The struggle between the adherents of the two languages affected every aspect of national life and was capable of instituting riots and overthrowing governments. The conflict still reigns, but today educated Greeks have realised the difficulty of replacing a living language by a dead one and that, as a result of improvement in standards of education, the ordinary people tend to avoid both the use of the more 'common' expressions and the old forms of ancient or foreign derivation. A certain gulf nevertheless still exists and is well illustrated in the press where the political news is printed in the official language and the serialised stories and the more popular items in the demotic tongue.

The language question has deeply affected Rhodian life this century. Apart from the problem of conflicting forms of Greek, the Italians openly discouraged, and often brutally suppressed, its use in any form. In 1912, Italian was declared the official language of the island and attempts to curb the teaching of Greek in schools were common. Children were ordered to speak Italian both in and out of school and public notices requested visitors to Rhodes to use Italian rather than Greek. After 1937, the Greek language, like Turkish, was taught optionally for two or three hours a week and there was no Greek taught at all in the lower classes. This was most significant in view of the small number of children who only just managed to pass beyond the elementary stage of education and hence had no opportunity for the academic study of the mother tongue. Allusions to Greece in schools were also censored and it was common for teachers who ignored these dictates to be imprisoned or deported. The Greek education system had been tied to the ideals of ancient Hellenism and to those of the Orthodox faith, and education in traditional subjects, especially religious instruction, had always been the principal care of the church. The replacement of Orthodox teaching in schools by the teachings of the Roman Church and the prohibition of Greek history and the study of the Greek language cut at the very roots of tradition.

As is to be expected, some of the older Rhodian population offer Italian as an alternative language. The universal language, however, is Greek and although some variation in dialect is found between Rhodes and the Greek mainland, nowhere does one come across incomprehensible Greek. A rich fund of local words and expressions exist and many of these emanate from Turkish. Turkish terms are particularly common in the kitchen and household vocabulary, especially in the names of dishes and meals.

GOVERNMENT AND ADMINISTRATION

The institution of local self-government has its roots deep in the traditions of the Greek people and the Rhodians are no exception. The islander willingly accepts the responsibilities of local government which in many ways is a development of the prevailing independence of the ancient city states. Under the Turks much of the government and administration was in the hands of the Greeks and only towards the end of the nineteenth century did this begin to change. The Italians, however, dissolved local municipalities and replaced them by state commissioners and the Rhodians were given the legal status of Italian-protected subjects without political rights. On union with Greece the island became part of a highly centralised government system with most of the initiative in local affairs coming from Athens.

Administratively, Rhodes is part of the *nomarchy* or prefecture of the Dodecanese which is a subdivision of the *dhiamerisma* or province of the Aegean Islands. Rhodes is the seat of the *nomarch* (prefect) and the territory is subdivided into four *eparchies* based on the islands of Kalymnos, Kos, Karpathos and Rhodes. The *eparchy* of Rhodes includes the neighbouring islands of Simi, Tilos, Alimnia and Kastellorizzo.

The *nomarch*, like the government officials of justice, education, agriculture, finance and public works etc, is appointed from Athens. Generally he is a competent and well-trained administrator representing central government, and his office is superior to all other authorities in the *nomarchy*. His duties include the maintenance of public order and security, the supervision of hospitals and detention centres and the upkeep of communications. In addition the *nomarch* enforces education acts, collects rates and taxes and administers government funds. He may be appointed as a career *nomarch* or as a political appointee so that changes in central government do not necessarily result in changes in *nomarch*. In the *eparchies* the functions and duties of the *nomarch* are carried out by his appointed representatives.

At the local, village, level the Rhodian is less impotent in affairs which concern his welfare more closely. Each village elects its own president (*proedros*) and community council under the system of proportional representation. A settlement with at least 300 inhabitants and a school is legally entitled to form such a *kinotsis*. The president is an unpaid official who acts as combination of mayor, counsellor, and chairman of all local activities. He is assisted by a secretary who is generally the local priest or schoolteacher. The formal activities of the *kinotsis* include the maintenance of statistics on population and village property, and the preparation of community tax rolls based on land tenure, produce and livestock ownership. The council can formulate plans for the improvement of the village community, but all decisions have to be approved by the *nomarch* who visits rural districts regularly and can plead the case to the government minister responsible.

The *kinotsis*, however, provides neither autonomy in village affairs, nor a unified structure. Governmental, commercial and educational activities are ultimately controlled from Athens and from the point of view of the political system and legal code etc, Rhodes is in all essentials identical with the rest of Greece. The police also belong to the national force, though the rank and file are usually Rhodians. Tourist police operate in Rhodes city.

FAMILY AND SOCIAL LIFE

The focal point in ordinary Rhodian life has long been the family and the local community it inhabits. Although old ways are gradually dying out, parochial ties and attitudes are very marked and family loyalties take precedence over all others. Greek society starts with the family and extends outward from it. Work and play, eating, conversation and celebration are all centred round the family unit.

Close traditional ties exist between the family and the land it farms, even where it is not strictly freehold. This association, inherited from early times, is responsible for the social structure of the Rhodian peasantry. The Italians, under various pretexts, attempted to break this association and derange the traditional structure of the family unit. It was common that farmers were prevented from cleaning their fallows, and then forced off their lands for neglecting their fields. Forced sales and expropriated lands for afforestation, military use and for settling Italian immigrants also separated families from inherited properties.

Both the Greek laws of inheritance and village custom require that property be divided equally among all heirs, sons and daughters alike, and that the latter are entitled to their share at marriage in the form of a dowry. This system of equal inheritance is at the base of many of the agricultural difficulties facing the island at present. Fields have been sub-divided into uneconomic units, often measuring a fraction of an acre, and reconsolidation is necessary before effective use can be made of mechanised farm implements and fertilisers. One traditional solution to the problem is the training or education of 'surplus' children for non-farming occupations. Education expenses are often counted as part of the inheritance and, as such, an heir will receive only a token share of the father's land. A second solution, well known in the history of Rhodes, has been emigration.

The dowry system is equally problematic. Until recently arranged marriages, with great stress on the dowry, were the rule and are still common. Although the daughter has now some say in the matter it is usually the father alone who has the responsibility for conducting the negotiations. The dowry itself comprises of household furniture, mattresses, linen, blankets and clothing and in some cases land is a necessary prerequisite and sometimes livestock. Money, however, is becoming a more common demand in villages as it has long been in the city. This money may represent years of family saving or it may have been partly earned by the girl herself in service or factory, or from the sale of her portion of the father's land. Today the dowry system is no longer so strict but it is still governed by complex points of procedure and ritual. For example, the obligation for the eldest son to see all sisters married before himself is still considered a point of honour in many families.

It is this sense of honour and self-esteem that is basic to the Rhodian character. To the Greek it is known as *philotimo* and governs both his status within a family, village and district and, second to none, his nationalism. The love of freedom rests heavily on *philotimo* and the Greek will go to great lengths to retain independence of action and thought. Nonchalance, improvisation, courage and the tendency to take unnecessary risks, all stem from this. It was for reasons of *philotimo* that, during the nineteenth century, many Rhodians joined the War of Independence on the Greek mainland to fight for the freedom of their country. It gave the Rhodians a great sense of independence to defy both the Turks and the Italians, in the sure knowledge that reprisal measures would be taken. The morale of the people was upheld by the belief that their freedom had not been forfeited and children who risked their lives to do unnecessary things such as defacing Mussolini posters and Fascist propaganda were merely giving expression to their essential independence. To the Rhodian, external coercion without submission had no bearing on the maintenance of *philotimo*.

Traditional Greek hospitality, which is a byword among foreigners, also rests on *philotimo*. It is a matter of honour and pride to welcome visitors and hospitality can reach overwhelming, even aggressive, proportions. It is on such occasions that other national characteristics of the Greeks reveal themselves, including their inquisitiveness and passion for conversation and noise. Social life takes place largely out of doors and this is as much a reflection of the Greek's love of crowds and their abhorrence of solitude as of an ideal climate for open-air relaxation. The house, as in ancient times, is little more than a place in which to sleep and life is conducted in the streets, the squares and, above all, in the cafés. The traditional café (*kafeneion*) is an important institution and predominantly a man's world. It acts as both local club and 'political' forum and hours are spent in talking, reading newspapers and watching the world go by. Much business, however, is also transacted in the café, appointments are kept and the latest news, political and commercial, is exchanged and discussed. In villages the café is the main social institution where the local inhabitants meet to discuss agricultural problems and community affairs. Other café occupations include a board game (*tavli*), which is backgammon, and the constant manipulation of strings of beads. These are the *komboloia* or worry-beads, a legacy from the Turks. They have no religious significance.

Although the Greeks are a practical and materialistic people they know the secret of amusing themselves with little or no money, and with little or no alcoholic stimulation. Many of the new forms of entertainment in Rhodes city are western-inspired and are geared to the annual influx of tourists. The average Rhodian has undemanding tastes and derives great pleasure from the simple things of life, chiefly sitting, talking and watching at a pavement café. Even less expensive is the pleasure of strolling in groups along certain stretches of the city's or village's main street. This is the *peripato* or *volta*, a characteristic feature of Rhodian life and a complex social ritual for those involved. The promenade takes place at given hours, usually in the early evening and is punctuated by stops at cafés or restaurants. For the native Rhodian the chief form of organised entertainment is that associated with religious feasts and holidays.

FESTIVALS AND FOLKLORE

On Rhodes the borderline between religion and folklore is particularly ill-defined. As elsewhere in Greece, religious feast-days and festivals are an important part of the Orthodox calendar and they have been maintained with all the pomp and circumstance of Byzantine ritual. Hardly a day passes on Rhodes without a celebration in honour of someone or something and each village pays homage to its patron saint with impressive services and popular fairs. Many of these local saints are names without a pedigree and the mystery surrounding their lives, entangled in legend and fragments of contemporary history, is known only to the villagers. The local feasts, known as the *paniyiri*, provide a focus of interest for the entire village and they are a glorious mixture of piety, trading, folklore and merry-making. It has often been said that the 'little saint of local fame keeps the broad current of Greek life flowing in the right direction'.

Religious ritual incorporates much of local origin and in rural areas, in particular, it is interwoven with superstitious and even pagan beliefs. These remain all-pervading forces on the island and belief in the evil eye and in the prophetic power of dreams is widespread. Other superstitions are deeply held convictions, especially those surrounding pregnancy and birth, although many peasant remedies reveal shrewd medical knowledge.

It is common that the various powers and attributes of the ancient gods and demigods of mythology have become embodied in Christian saints, as for example St Demetrius who has inherited the characteristics of Demeter, the goddess of plenty. The patron saint of sailors is St Nicholas who has replaced Poseidon, the sea god; St Artemidos has supplanted ancient Artemis, goddess of the hunt, and St Dionysius stands for Dionysus, the pagan god of wine. The infiltration of pagan mythology into Christian folklore is well illustrated at Lindos. The sacred grotto below the acropolis is still venerated by the local population, though the Virgin Mary (*Panaghia*) has supplanted the maiden goddess Athena. To the Greeks, the Virgin not only possesses a cure for all human evils, but also, when necessity calls, takes on the attributes of the war goddess Athena as the protectress of Hellenism in times of want and disaster.

Other villages have their superstitious customs that parade under the cloak of religion. At Koskinou, and elsewhere, on the eve of St John the Baptist's Day (24 June), dried May Day wreaths which adorn doors and gates are ceremoniously piled into the streets to burn. Jumping through the flames is considered a token of purification. Rhodes too, like the rest of Greece, has clung to its belief in Pan, who half-man, half-goat, is a small edition of the devil. The Orthodox Church is partial to the association and a visitation by the creature can lead to things like kidnapping, miscarriages and the souring of milk! According to superstition, intercourse on 25 March will result in the child being born on Christmas Eve and this child will inevitably turn out to be a Pan.

Religious relics and icons are highly venerated objects of local churches and many of them are claimed to have miraculous powers. A festival is held at Kremasti between 15 and 20 August which is counted as one of the greatest in the Dodecanese. It

Page 125   (above) Barren rocky ground and simple farmsteads are typical of the agricultural scene around Lindos; (below) the ubiquitous goat grazes the maquis, but is often penned at night

(*above*) Peasant women gathering firewood near the village of Siana; (*below*) sponges for sale at a stall in the town of Rhodes

celebrates the Virgin of Kremasti, a now-faded memorial to the powers of Our Lady of Philerimos, the famous miracle-working icon of the Middle Ages which is said to have accompanied the Knights to Malta. The festival of the *Panaghia*, or the Assumption of Our Lady, is held on 15 August, and the days following are celebrated in feasting, singing and dancing. Another festival that attracts wide crowds is held on 30 July at Soroni in celebration of St Soulas, a reputed fellow passenger of St Paul. Soulas, in all probability, is a corruption of Saul and is a case of transferred attributes. Lawrence Durrell in his book, *Reflections on a Marine Venus*, has a graphic tragicomic account of the events of the annual festival which include donkey and horse racing.

August is the most important month for festivals. Expert village dance groups tour the island and Rhodes is visited by similar groups from Kos, Simi and Kasos. The villages of Maritsa, Kalithies, Trianda, Kremasti and Embona hold dance displays throughout the month. Many of the dances have lost their regional characteristics, but like folklore, they are deeply rooted in mythology. Also universally celebrated is 8 September. It marks the name-day of the Virgin Mary and throughout the island barren women pray and often make pilgrimage to the monastery on Mount Tsambika. It should be noted that birthdays are rarely celebrated by the Greeks, but rather the name-days of the saints after whom the majority of Greeks are named or can trace some contact. An important day for the countless Marys on Rhodes is 15 August.

Easter is the most important festival in the Orthodox calendar, but even this seems to have been grafted on to what was probably Lesser Eleusinia in ancient times—the return of Persephone and the general awakening of nature after the winter months. It is the period of red eggs and roasted lamb and is ushered in by forty days of fasting. The two Sundays before Lent are known respectively as Meat Sunday and Cheese Sunday. The week between them is celebrated with carnivals and masquerades reminiscent of the Old Cronia festivals of antiquity. Scholars suggest that Lent itself commemorates Demeter's long abstinence from food during her search for her lost daughter.

The Greek Orthodox Easter is calculated in a complicated manner and together with Whitsun its date is still based on the Julian-style calendar and occurs anything up to a month later than in Western Christendom. Easter involves as much preparation in the kitchen as Christmas does in Western Europe and work starts about ten days before the event. In the villages, houses and even streets, receive their annual coat of whitewash and rich and poor alike feast on Paschal Lamb. On Maundy Thursday the lamb is killed and hung throughout Good Friday until Saturday when *mayeritsa*, the Easter Soup, is prepared from the liver, lungs, heart and entrails of the young lamb. Universal mourning reaches a climax in the evening of Good Friday when every church holds a funeral procession. The flower-covered symbolical bier of Christ is followed by the clergy, church dignitaries and the general population. On Saturday the long church service ends with rejoicing, the lighting of candles and fireworks, and Easter Sunday is celebrated in eating, drinking, and dancing. Preparations for the midday feast begin very early. In many villages a shallow trench is dug and filled with glowing charcoal. A spit, or *souvla* as it is called, is arranged over the fire and the whole lamb is slowly turned by hand for several hours and basted with lemon juice and olive oil. The pomp, ceremony and feasting varies from church to church and village to village, but even the humblest rural community celebrates Easter with great dedication.

Christmas is not so enthusiastically celebrated as in western countries though there are traditional rites on Christmas eve, including incense burning before supper and the eating of flat buns called 'Christ's loaves'. Present giving is associated with the New Year which is St Basil's Day. A cake containing a silver coin is made and luck belongs to whoever gets the coin. After supper the family plays games of divination to determine what the coming year will bring.

The chief national and non-religious festivals are 25 March, which is Independence Day and 28 October which throughout Greece is popularly called 'Ochi Day'. 'Ochi' means 'No' and the date celebrates 1940 when Greece rejected Mussolini's ultimatum to surrender and entered the war on the side of the Allies.

POPULATION STRUCTURE

The demographic development of Rhodes has been radically influenced by the political events of this century. Prior to the Italian occupation of the island there were no trustworthy estimates and the first census of 1912, which recorded a total population of 45,000, was not accurate in detail. Subsequent figures were more precise and coherent but were still complicated by migration and refugee movements.

The island today is not densely populated, though throughout this century the population has been increasing. From the 1912 estimate it grew to 54,818 in 1931, to 61,252 in 1937 and to 68,873 in 1961. This latter figure, however, appears insignificant when it is remembered that in antiquity the city of Rhodes alone was developed to house a population of 80,000–100,000 inhabitants. During the course of history many islanders emigrated to the Greek mainland and to other parts of the eastern Mediterranean. Although there have been compensating periods of repatriation most authorities would agree that there is not room for a much larger population, even under the artificial economic conditions now stemming from tourism.

Between 1951 and 1961 the population increase averaged 5·6 per cent per annum but there was a distinction between the rural population (40,754 in 1961) which declined by 0·42 per cent and the urban population of Rhodes city which increased by 15·81 per cent, that is from 24,280 in 1951 to 28,119 in 1961. The island, like the whole of Greece, suffers from migratory problems, both rural-urban movement and emigration. Between 1951 and 1961, 6,243 people left the island of which 5,037 were from rural areas. The problem, however, is not so acute as in other Aegean islands and the age structure and male–female ratio is relatively well balanced. In 1961, 34·08 per cent of the population was under 15 years of age, 57·80 per cent in the 15–64 age group and 8·12 per cent above 65. The high urban increase is related chiefly to the economic development of the capital area, particularly its tourist industry.

7 THE RHODIAN ECONOMY

THE contemporary Rhodian economy suffers and benefits from the island's long and chequered history. Oppression by alien conquerors, devastation of natural resources and the lack of capital for improvements and equipment have all contributed to reduce the fertility of the island. In some respects the damage is irreparable especially when it has concerned the removal of the natural vegetation cover and the consequent effect on soil erosion. The economy, however, continues to benefit from the scientific management first introduced by the Italians. Agricultural improvement, road-making, port reconstruction, and the initiation of a tourist industry are all aspects of development upon which the island has become increasingly dependent since its union with Greece.

As an integral part of the Greek state the Rhodian economy is inseparably tied to that of Greece and decisions made in Athens, whether economic or political, have direct repercussions on the island. For this reason it is perhaps unwise to single out the Rhodian economy and to review it in isolation from the rest of the country. This chapter may be defended on the grounds that Rhodes epitomises the general economic characteristics of Greece as a whole and, as such, offers an interesting case study of the development problems common to the country.

Rhodian agriculture, in spite of significant innovations in its management and operation, is still lacking in technical progress and modern methods. Demographic pressure on available agricultural land, together with traditional ideas on ownership and inheritance, have resulted in intense farm fragmentation and inefficient methods of production. The manufacturing sector is also underdeveloped and the majority of the labour force is employed in extremely small-scale, low-productivity firms which are heavily dependent on agriculture for their raw materials. These major characteristics present in microcosm some of the current development problems of Greece, but Rhodes, like the rest of the country, is now increasingly dependent on tourism which provides the island with hard currency beneficial to its balance of payments. Since the tourist industry is concentrated on Rhodes city, socio-economic inequalities are widening between the capital and the rest of the island and this is reflected in population movement away from rural areas. What exists on Rhodes at a local level finds its larger counterpart in the economic and social inequalities common between Athens and provincial Greece.

AGRICULTURE

The Rhodian economy is basically agrarian, and although the island may be regarded as one of the most fertile and productive in the Aegean, it nevertheless suffers from the same major problems facing Greek agriculture in general. The dissected relief of much of the island and active gully erosion ensures that agricultural land is in short supply, 70,450 acres or 17·2 per cent of the island's area is classified as cultivable, and a further 125,977 acres (32·05 per cent) as pasture. These acreages support a rural population of 40,754 (60 per cent of the island's total population).

The generalised land utilisation map (Fig 18) indicates a far higher proportion of the island under cultivation. It should be stressed, however, that of the areas registered as arable land, approximately one-tenth only is intensively cultivated and furthermore a large proportion of it lies fallow each year. Slope and altitude greatly restrict cultivation and in many parts of the island farming has extended beyond the limits consistent

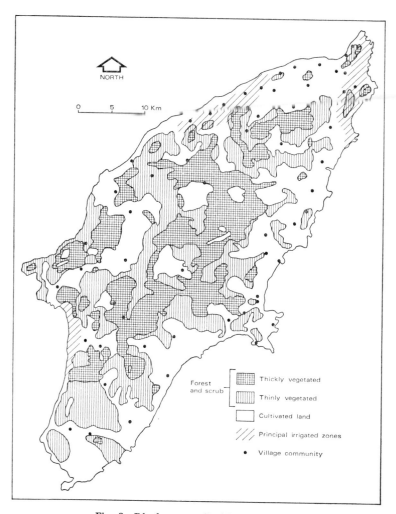

NORTH

0   5   10 Km

Forest
and scrub

Thickly vegetated

Thinly vegetated

Cultivated land

Principal irrigated zones

• Village community

Fig 18   Rhodes, generalised land utilisation

with economic and conservational land use. Soil erosion is a common problem and is the result of centuries of misuse and mismanagement. One of its main causes is the erratic and heavy winter rainfall, but it has been accentuated by reckless deforestation and over-grazing, especially by the omnivorous goat.

Terracing is one method, long used to combat erosion and to increase the arable acreage. Terraces are constructed from the ample material provided by the rocky subsoil and they are filled with soil from alluvial valley bottoms. The root systems of the olive and carob help to consolidate the terrace for grains and other crops which are cultivated between these and other fruit trees. The scarcity of water, resulting from seasonal rainfall and steep run-off, is also diminished by terracing and where possible water shortages are compensated locally by irrigation and well water. It is surprising, however, that only 1·58 per cent of the cultivated area is irrigated and is confined to parts of the north-east and north-west coasts and to the area around the Gulf of Apolakkion in the south-west (Fig 18).

Problems of a sociological, technical and economic nature also beset Rhodian agriculture and aggravate the physical restrictions. The land-tenure system and the persistence of dowry and inheritance laws have greatly hindered agricultural advancement and it is only relatively recently that such anachronisms have been tackled with any consistency. Moslem land laws survived into this century and still continue in part, though under the Italian administration they were progressively modified and simplified. Inheritance laws and the equal division of land among descendants has meant a steady reduction in size and the fragmentation of holdings, and only the occasional spate of reconsolidation, usually following the arrival of a new regime, has helped to counter this trend. Local custom, however, has always triumphed over these spasmodic attempts and the pattern on Rhodes remains one of very small holdings, on average approximately 3 acres per farmer, consisting of a number of fragmented parcels scattered around the village.

Kasperon noted that the largest single plot encountered during field investigation in the Dodecanese was one of 15 acres in Rhodes. Such sizes are extremely rare and in all Rhodian villages a single plot of 2–5 acres is considered large.

Under the Italian regime a bold attempt was made to place Rhodian agriculture on a competitive basis. An intensive campaign was mounted to increase the use of fertilisers and agricultural machinery and research stations were responsible for the study of plant pests and diseases and for the introduction and acclimatisation of new plant species and varieties. A large-scale model farm with Italian personnel was set up at Kattavia, together with institutes of experimental farming at Rhodes and Paradission. Attention was also given to land reclamation, drainage and the improvement of backward upland areas. The metal windmill, still a feature of the north-west coast, was another Italian innovation, introduced to tap deep water supplies for irrigation purposes.

The Italian farming methods and improvements were received with passive resistance by the Rhodian farmers and only slowly was curiosity aroused and imitation stimulated. Trained Italian immigrant farmers were given expropriated land for the explicit purpose of setting a good example to the Rhodians. The immigration was carefully organised and subsidised by Azienda associations similar to those of the Po Valley and Roman Campagna. The Malona area, one of the richest farming areas on the island, was settled largely by Sienese labourers and it became an important centre for Italian farming.

On union with Greece the islanders, naturally, inherited the benefits of the Italian agricultural improvements and the opening up of Greek mainland markets stimulated production. Better communications, both by sea and air, have made the island aware of wider markets, but although great changes have taken place in Rhodian agriculture, the basic problems remain the same. The need for farm consolidation is paramount, for in a system where small and fragmented plots operate, valuable time and effort is wasted travelling to and from fields. But differences in the quality of land plots and their trees, together with nostalgic values derived from a long history of family ownership, appear as strong arguments against attempts at redistribution. Fragmentation also mitigates the application of modern production methods, of mechanisation and of better drainage, irrigation and conservation. The use of chemical fertilisers is still unsatisfactory despite the fact that their marketing and distribution is now controlled by the Agricultural Bank. On average, Rhodes uses 3·4kg of fertiliser per acre as compared with 5–8kg in parts of the Peloponnesus and Crete, and even these latter figures are exceptionally low by Western European standards. The heaviest application of artificial fertiliser is made to vegetables, vines, melons and tobacco. In terms of farm mechanisation, Rhodes compares favourably with much of Greece, but still inadequately with Western Europe.

Experts who have studied the problems of Greek agriculture are agreed that improvement is best tackled through a number of major channels and the suggestions are equally valid for Rhodes. The most significant of these are changes in the organisational and institutional bases of farming, in particular the modernisation of agricultural co-operatives to which the majority of farmers belong, improvements in crop and animal yields through the use of better varieties, a more intensive use of fertilisers, a speeding-up of mechanisation and land-reclamation schemes, and the extension of an intensified programme of agricultural research and education.

MAJOR CROPS

An increasing specialisation in market-orientated products has tended to break down the traditional crop complex of grains, olives and vines. These, however, still form the basis of the average islander's diet.

Grains

Wheat, alone, accounts for 20 per cent of the cultivated total and yields have shown a marked increase in recent years as a result of improved varieties of seed, the greater use of fertiliser and better techniques of production. Often regarded as the Mediterranean field crop *par excellence*, the well-known adaptability of wheat to a variety of soil and climatic conditions is thoroughly tested on Rhodes. Its cultivation ranges from the cooler and more humid mountain slopes to the hotter and drier coastal and interior plains. The grain is grown primarily for local consumption. The other important grain is barley, grown mainly as a winter crop and which has the advantage of maturing quickly. Like oats it is an important feed crop, though oats is less demanding in soil requirements. The concentration is on red oats which is relatively tolerant to high temperatures. Barley and oats account for about 12 per cent of the cultivated area, with the latter confined in the main to the poorer-favoured areas of the island. Minor cereal crops include maslin, millet and sorghum which are produced for livestock and poultry feed.

The Olive

The olive is the most significant fruit tree on Rhodes and it is of inestimable value to rural families. It is said that man can live off the olive tree and the ancient Greeks well knew their indebtedness to the olive harvest. Preserved in brine and their own oil, olives form, with bread and goat's milk, the basic sustenance of the working people. Crushed, the fruit gives oil which, in its refined form, is both a food and a cooking medium of nutritive value. The residue of the oil is boiled down for soap and the remaining pulp returns to the land as a fertiliser or is used as fuel for the domestic fire. The services of the tree do not end with the fruit and the oil it produces. The annual pruning provides fodder and bedding for sheep and goats; the hard, close-grained timber from the heavier branches is material for dwellings, furniture, tools and utensils; and the waste wood provides fuel for warmth and cooking. In the past the olive was also suited to the political situation of the island. If farmers were forced to abandon a grainfield or a vineyard for any length of time, the possibility of its being ruined by lack of care was high, whereas an olive grove would suffer little damage.

There are an estimated 750,000 olive trees on Rhodes and often they form serried ranks on land that is interploughed for grains. Intercropping is a common practice and on occasion olives are cultivated along with vines and vegetables. The trees grow under marked climatic restraints but there is a wide freedom of choice in terms of terrain and soil conditions. In many parts of the island the olive flourishes on what otherwise would be uncultivated and uneconomic land, and often it is seen growing wild among maquis or in natural olive groves. The major control is satisfactory drainage. The mature tree develops an extensive root system which makes it resistant to drought.

The main olive-producing areas are found in the north and extensive groves surround the villages of Trianda, Aphandou, Archangelos and Malona. Improvements in tending and harvesting are now common but some primitive methods still exist, such as shaking the branches to harvest the crop. Major factors contributing to irregular and low yields include a relatively high proportion of old trees, nitrogen deficiency, imperfect pruning and unsatisfactory pest and disease control. On average, around 15,000 tons are produced for oil and 500 tons for the table, annually.

The Vine

On Rhodes, viticulture is also a traditional agricultural pursuit and its origins can be traced back into antiquity. This intensively exploited branch of agricultural activity produces table grapes, sultana raisins and wine grapes. The latter, which occupy around 7 per cent of the cultivated area, tend to be the more important and the manufacture of red and white wine is an old-established Rhodian industry. The sultana raisin was introduced from Asia Minor in the nineteenth century but its cultivation can in no way compete with the great currant- and sultana-producing areas of Crete and the Peloponnesus. About 250 tons of sultanas are produced annually and an equivalent tonnage of table grapes. Vines on Rhodes are grown as bushes with no artificial support. They usually occupy flat or undulating land, preferably with deep, fertile soils. At lower altitudes many are planted under olive trees.

Other Fruit Trees

With the exception of the olive and the vine the most copious tree crops are the carob, fig and citrus fruits. The carob is a small evergreen tree found throughout the Mediterranean. It has long pods which are rich in sugar and protein and is used as animal fodder, human food and for the fermentation of beverages. In addition, a gum made from the pods is utilised in paper-making and tobacco-curing, as a stabiliser in food products and as a celluloid in photographic supplies. The carob generally grows on wasteland and in spite of its many uses it is used on Rhodes principally as a fodder crop.

The fig is also well adapted to stony ground and thrives without irrigation. The first crop in June and July is mostly eaten fresh. The second and sweeter crop (August to October), is generally preferred for drying. The Soroni district has long been famous for its fig harvests. In contrast to the carob and fig, the lemon, orange and citron demand much more care in cultivation and require special soil and climatic conditions. They flourish in the sheltered districts of the island. Since they require abundant water, their growth is largely restricted to the irrigated areas. There is a concentration on citrus production on the east coast between the villages of Archangelos and Masari where the alluvial soils are fertile and well drained.

Irrigated orange and lemon groves are also common around Malona.

Vegetables

In recent years Rhodian agriculture has shown an increasing tendency to specialise in garden produce and other market-orientated crops. Most of the market and nursery gardens are found in the vicinity of Rhodes city where fresh vegetables give good returns even on quite small holdings. In the main they are related to the areas of light Quaternary soils and the chief irrigated districts. Considerable quantities are exported to the Greek mainland. Over 6 per cent of the total cultivated area is now devoted to spring vegetables and the chief early crops are green beans, tomatoes and cucumbers. The northern coast, around Trianda, is intensively laid out in vegetable plots which are protected by bamboo windbreaks.

Other specialities of the island are melons and water-melons which prosper in many lowland areas. Neither are specific in terms of soil and climatic requirements, though yields are greatly increased through irrigation.

ANIMAL HUSBANDRY

In spite of the fact that 32 per cent of the island is officially classified as pasture, animal husbandry and mixed farming have never been as significant to the Rhodian economy as cultivation. Each farm-owning household, however, maintains some live-stock—one or two horses or cattle, a mule or donkey and some sheep and goats. Chickens and pigs are also an additional source of livelihood and income. In 1961 there were 46,154 goats, 28,235 sheep, 7,972 cattle, 6,583 donkeys, 2,319 pigs, 1,051 mules and 823 horses on the island.

In general, Rhodian pasture supports a sparse cover of annual grasses and a meagre but varied growth of annual and perennial legumes. Shrubs but trees provide much of the feed from natural pasture and a large proportion of it is confined to deforested and eroded land, the product of long-continued over-grazing. Maquis and scrub, fallow and stubble, orchards and vineyards, in fact all land that is not directly under cultivation provides some sort of natural pasture, though generally it is of low quality.

The traditional pastoral activities are the rearing of sheep and goats. During the Turkish period it was common for shepherds and their families to migrate to Anatolia where better pastures could often be found during certain months of the year. Today, the flocks and herds range widely, but they observe territorial boundaries and are usually tended and penned in a fold at night. Breeding sheep for one particular line of production has never been generally practised. The breed belongs to a hardy mountain variety capable of surviving the rigours of Rhodian pasturage and climate and they provide meat, milk, fat and wool, usually for local consumption. The short and coarse wool is suitable only for carpets and inferior domestic products. Sheep's milk is rarely drunk in liquid form, but yoghourt and a variety of cheeses are prepared. Goats occupy the wilder sections of the island and thrive in places where other types of livestock would fail. They are raised for meat and milk, and goat's cheese is a staple of the rural diet.

Traditionally the shepherds and goatherds form a class apart and it has been common to lease flocks from farmers, the tenders receiving part of the increase for their services. In the sheep and goat is illustrated something of the paradox confronting the Rhodian rural economy—while being a mainstay of a way of life, they nevertheless devastate the landscape in a way that has serious repercussions on other forms of agricultural activity.

Cattle are becoming more common on Rhodes. In the past, hot summers made grazing difficult and the cost of irrigated fodder was prohibitive. Cattle were used as subsistence animals and as beasts of burden for ploughing and transportation.

Recently, the rapid expansion of the island's tourist industry has created a demand for fresh dairy produce and better-quality meat and it is significant that 14·27 per cent of the cultivated area is now devoted to fodder crops. The Greek government pays bonuses for fodder crops and two-thirds of those grown on Rhodes are for hay.

Above and below the limits of normal village agriculture are the subsidiary resources of forestry and fishing. On Rhodes, 'forest' covers roughly 156,000 acres but its definition is a broad one and includes maquis and sparse strands of small and often uneconomic trees. From a commercial point of view forests suffer from drastic limitations and provide relatively meagre supplies of timber for low uses such as fuel. Exploitation is also impaired by poor access facilities. The Italian administration attempted to conserve all forested areas capable of improvement, but forest-land is still subject to grazing, often in contravention of state forestry-protection regulations, and regeneration is impaired. Devastation by goatherds and by fire to increase the pasture area has resulted, today, in forest products having only a minor and local significance. On average Rhodes produces 20,000 tons of wood annually, mainly for fuel purposes, and 200 tons of charcoal.

Fishing is a common livelihood, but most regular fishermen, in addition, usually cultivate a smallholding. The Dodecanese islands as a whole produce about 4,000 tons of fish annually and in the past sponge-fishing was a major occupation and still employs considerable numbers in the islands of Simi and Kalymnos. Rhodes never participated fully in sponge-fishing although it was organised from the island after 1936 with the establishment of the *Societa Anonima degli Spugne di Rodi*. Today, the most common sea products are octopus, squid, 'lobster' (astakos or crawfish), mullet, crayfish and rock-fish, but the

Page 143 (above) An improvised table for backgammon in the market at Rhodes; (below) a typical range of Rhodian souvenirs in the old bazaar quarter of the walled town

Page 144 (*above*) Carpet-making, employing female labour, is a thriving industry at Aphandou; (*below*) hand-painted pottery in traditional island styles finds ready markets in the tourist shops of Rhodes and Greece

equipment of the fishing fleet reflects the backwardness of this industry.

MANUFACTURING INDUSTRY

Out of an active population of 26,800 (1961), only 14·38 per cent, or 3,854 persons were engaged in manufacturing activities and allied trades such as building construction, gas, water, electricity and sewage disposal. As should be evident from these figures the presence and impact of industry is rather feeble in the Rhodian economic scene and visitors might well leave the island without having been aware of a factory. The reasons are not hard to find. The lack of raw materials, with the exception of sands, clays and stone, shortages of capital and power, the absence of available technical education and narrow markets, have combined to restrain and inhibit the development of a manufacturing sector. These factors, which are unlikely to disappear in the near future, make it improbable, or inconceivable, that factory industry will, for many years, have a dominant part to play in the Rhodian economy.

A breakdown of manufacturing into its respective branches, and in order of importance, is given below.

	Numbers employed	Percentage of total
Food and beverages	985	25·55
Footwear	830	21·87
Metal products	449	11·65
Textiles	430	11·15
Wood products	381	9·88
Non-metallic mineral products	303	7·86
Paper, printing, etc	99	2·56
Chemicals	62	1·60
Others	315	7·88
Total	3,854	100·00

As one would expect, manufacturing activity is mainly concentrated in and around Rhodes city where the dominant feature is the existence of a large number of small firms, many of which are characterised by handicraft methods and operate at less-than-optimum scales of production. Small establishments catering for the souvenir and tourist market are particularly common, and these and the traditions behind them, are discussed in detail in Chapter 8. In 1961 the island had only 6 establishments employing more than 50 workers—a total of 603 workers in all. The food-processing industries, heavily dependent on local agricultural products, have established a useful, perhaps a growing place. Specialisation lies in the canning of fruit and vegetables for export and Paradission has a canning factory which handles some of the produce grown in the area. Olive oil of good quality is also refined for export and the low-grade oil is used for soap-making, an industry first introduced by the Italians. Macaroni and pasta, flour-milling, bakeries and biscuit factories, together with the confection of sweets, jams and cakes are the other main food industries. High-grade wines are also manufactured and exported from the island, and are famous throughout Greece, as are a number of dessert wines manufactured from raisins. With these food industries may be grouped those devoted to preparing natural products such as hides, skins, wool and dried fish. The small tobacco industry relies on both local and imported brands.

The footwear industry is largely of the workshop variety and again relies on local and imported raw materials. Like textiles it illustrates a peculiar supply–demand relationship concerned with the satisfaction of local needs for low-quality products. Exceptions in both cases are items for tourist traffic. In Rhodes city and in Archangelos quality hide and soft goatskin boots are made. Woollen, linen and cotton textiles are still woven on domestic looms, with homespun yarn, and intended predominantly for the local market. European goods, however, are now the main textile products and even silk, an ancient industry, has suffered from severe competition. By Western standards the island has no heavy industry and the metal goods category includes, in the main, the assembly of machines and appliances, chiefly bicycles and household goods. The non-metallic mineral industries refer to brick-making, cement-making, tile-making and ceramics.

TOURISM

Whereas manufacturing industry suffers from a number of problems and deficiencies the same cannot be said for the tourist industry. The modern invaders of Rhodes are the holiday-makers and catering for their needs has become the fastest-growing sector of the economy and a prime source of revenue and livelihood. Tourism has repercussions on almost every branch of economic activity and has become an effective means of forging new developments in building construction, transportation, agriculture and in a whole range of personal and commercial services.

As a holiday centre Rhodes goes as near to being all things to all men as any Greek island can. It boasts an inexhaustible wealth of natural and historical attractions and for the relaxation and comfort of the modern traveller the capital is well equipped with hotels of every category, restaurants, bars, nightclubs and even a casino. Many see Rhodes as fast developing as the Majorca of the Aegean but, although the number of tourists attracted solely by the island's climate and beaches is increasing, the presence of tangible manifestations of its earlier civilisations continues to be important. Statistics provided by the Greek National Tourist Organisation indicate Lindos to be the ninth most important archaeological site in Greece with an average of 24,000 people visiting the village and its acropolis annually.

The Italians were the first to realise the full tourist potential of the island and hotels, including the famous Hotel des Roses, and other amenities were built to encourage the trade. In the late twenties Kallithea Spa was built as a resort and watering-place for the treatment of rheumatism, arthritis, diabetic and kidney diseases, and lavish expenditure on public buildings and garden suburbs in Rhodes was an attempt to make it a show-place for the eastern Mediterranean. The Apolona area was also developed as a kind of subsidised summer resort for Italians. During the Italian occupation tourist traffic increased from 700 in 1922 to 40,000 in 1928 and 60,000 in 1934. These figures, however, are insignificant when compared with the 154,873 tourists accommodated in the island's hotels and pensions during 1970. A high percentage of these were Swedes and West Germans and during the summer Rhodes almost becomes a quasi-Swedish town. Swedish is spoken in a number of shops and many signboards and restaurant menus carry Swedish translations.

The National Tourist Organisation is now involved in an active campaign to promote winter tourism and Rhodes has been selected along with Athens and Crete as part of the experiment. During the winter season, 1971–2, some 40,000 beds were available on Rhodes and on the demand side the prospects appear encouraging. The NTO also organises festivals and displays of tourist appeal. During the summer the most successful have been the wine festival at Rhodini Park, classical dramas at the ancient theatre and son et lumière at the Palace of the Grand Master. The latter presentation is given in French, German, English, Swedish and Greek and reflects the major national constituents of the island's visitors.

Rhodes clearly has advantages in the tourist sector and the contribution of the industry to the island's income, employment and regional development has been considerable. The future rate of tourist growth will depend mainly on the ability of the supply side to respond, both quantitatively and qualitatively, to the demand.

THE CONSTRUCTION INDUSTRY

The construction industry has greatly profited from tourism. The new roads, bridges, apartment blocks and hotels have led to the expansion of ancillary services such as gas, electricity, telephone and water etc, which in turn has brought more work to the building trade. Private entrepreneurial activity is encouraged in the development of tourism and a number of special concessions and incentives are offered to investors and developers. Land speculation, however, especially around the capital, has led to the introduction of a number of restrictions to the purchase of large areas for building, especially by foreigners.

It should also be noted that property development in and around the city is a hazardous business. The Greek Archaeological Society keeps an ever-watchful eye on redevelopment in the hope that it will reveal further evidence relating to the early history of the city. It is common for work to be suspended until the authorities have examined new discoveries and heavy fines are imposed if relics are not reported. It has even been known for newly erected properties to be pulled down solely because they have been built on unreported Hellenistic or medieval foundations.

COMMUNICATIONS

Rhodes has no railways, but the island is served by a reasonably adequate road network (Fig 19). The Italians are principally responsible for the system which formed an integral part of their modernisation and development plan for the island. Prior to the Italian occupation, travel from Rhodes city to the interior, or from one village to another, was a matter of pack-mules or donkeys, with only a few stretches where wheeled transport was possible.

Fig 19   Rhodes, place-names and roads

Basically, the road network consists of eastern and western coastal routes which link Rhodes city with the principal rural settlements. The two routes beyond Lindos and Kalavarda are metalled highways and similar branch routes extend to Profitis Ilias, Epano Kalamon, Maritsa, Philerimos, Koskinou and Kallithies. The secondary routes are hard-packed dirt roads, which, by and large, are adequate, although they are dusty in

150

summer and wet in winter. The island is also served by numerous
trackways which connect the smaller rural centres. Along these,
connections between adjacent villages are often circuitous, but
it is still possible for motorised traffic to penetrate into the most
isolated parts of the island.

Buses hold the monopoly of the island passenger-transport
system and a good network of services is in operation. The two
bus companies, KTEL and RODA, operate from Rhodes city.
They are not competitive and have strictly interpreted agree-
ments as to the areas and settlements they serve. The former
operates in the eastern part of the island and the latter in the
western part and only in the extreme south do their services
overlap. The local buses are run exclusively for the convenience
of villagers and time-tables have been set up for the purpose
of taking them to markets in the morning and back in the
evening. Their timings, therefore, are often inconvenient for
the visitor.

The bus fleets are a mixture of modern vehicles and 'bone-
shakers'. They are always overcrowded and often unpunctual,
but they never fail to arrive at their destinations. KTEL operate
services to the southern villages of Kattavia and Messanagros
six times a week and the return journey is usually made the
following day. Lindos is the most frequently served centre by
KTEL with two or three daily services, returning the same day.
The RODA route from Rhodes to Kattavia via the principal
villages of Kremasti, Soroni, Kalavarda, Mandriko, Embona,
Aghios Issidoros, Monolithos and Apolakia, operates once a
week with the return journey again the following day. Another
once-weekly route goes as far as Arnitha and returns to Rhodes.
In the northern part of the island the frequency of services is
increased and the villages of Paradission, Kremasti, Trianda,
Aphandou and Archangelos have regular connections with
Rhodes. During the summer season fast services also connect the
city with the major tourist attractions such as ancient Cameiros
and Lindos. A large number of private tour operators also

organise excursions to the island's chief scenic and historical sites.

Rhodes city itself is served by a number of suburban bus routes and there is an adequate supply of taxis and self-drive cars. The Rhodians, like all Greeks, use taxis freely and even small villages generally support at least one cab. Usually it is some mammoth American model kept as much for prestige as for convenience. The number of vehicles crowding the island's roads has increased at a rapid rate in recent years, but the main concentration is around the capital where traffic jams can be severe. The principal coast roads, particularly from Archangelos and from Paradission, Kremasti and Trianda north to Rhodes city, have significantly heavy traffic, but throughout the remainder of the island traffic flow tends to be light.

The old town of Rhodes, with its narrow streets and restricted entries, is unsuited to modern traffic and is largely the domain of the bicycle and motor-cart. In Lindos, too, little more than mules and donkeys ply the streets, but even so a system of traffic regulations, including a speed limit, has often been suggested to govern these animals!

The advent of mass tourism has brought considerable improvement to the island's external communications and Rhodes is linked to Athens and other parts of Greece by regular air and boat services. From Piraeus one or more boats leave daily for Rhodes and are the major service links, bringing and collecting food, stores and post. The journey time varies according to the route taken and to the type of craft. It can vary from 13 to 33hr and time-tables often run late depending on the extent of loading and unloading at the various ports of call en route. Two scheduled steamer routes link Rhodes with Athens via Simi, Tilos, Kos, Kalymnos, Leros and Patmos and then by way of either the central or northern Cyclades islands. Another route connects the island with Athens via Karpathos, Kasos and Crete. Several shipping lines have cruise boats and passenger-carrying cargo vessels that call at Rhodes from Genoa,

Venice, Cyprus and Haifa. There are links between the island and Turkey and during summer an excursion operates to the Turkish port of Marmaris.

Within the last decade air travel has rapidly increased in popularity. Rhodes is linked to Athens by the domestic flights of Olympic Airways. The frequency is 5 services daily in winter and 6 daily in summer, commencing 1 June. Flight time varies between 43min and 1hr 10min, depending on the type of aircraft. In summer regular flights also link Rhodes with Iraklion and Salonica. At present the island is served by Maritsa Airport, 15km from Rhodes city, but in response to the unprecedented increase in tourist traffic a new terminal is under construction at Paradission.

Throughout summer direct air services operate between Rhodes and London, Nicosia, Paris, Rome, Cairo and Tel Aviv. Special chartered planes also carry passengers from West Germany and Scandinavian countries and Rhodes has air offices including BEA, Air France, Lufthansa, Sabena, Olympic and Cyprus Airways. Maritsa Airport handles, on average, 61,000 passengers annually, which makes it second to Athens (331,018 passengers) and Salonica (101,582) but closely followed by Iraklion (57,609).

TRADE

It was Italian policy to create in Rhodes a major centre of Levantine trade, thereby restoring the function it served in antiquity and to a lesser extent during the Middle Ages. The attempt to undermine the commercial advantages of Izmir never really paid off, even with the destruction of the city in 1922. Today, Rhodes is a medium-sized Greek port serving in the main the consumption needs of the island. In terms of average annual tonnage of goods handled (126,967) the port ranks as the nineteenth in size in Greece. It is the chief market for island produce for export and for imported goods destined

153

for redistribution among the Dodecanese. Major imports include wines and spirits, tobacco, chemicals, textiles, wood, paper, leather, vehicles, cereals and animal products. The principal exports are agricultural products, wine, oil and handicraft goods. In terms of passenger traffic, however, the port ranks as eighth in importance in Greece, handling on average 100,000 passengers annually of which a high proportion are international passengers.

As a trading and commercial centre Rhodes, and the Dodecanese as a whole, has a major advantage in that it is taxed at a rate markedly lower than that applying to the rest of Greece. In much the same way as Suleiman awarded the islands 'privileges', the Greek government in 1947 bestowed certain marks of honour on the Dodecanese which applied to personal taxation as well as to duty on goods. The period of reduced taxation was originally limited to ten years, but the concessions were extended and they remain in force today. This special arrangement means that many goods from all over the world can be purchased at a lower price than in their country of origin, although they are subject to a 4 per cent municipal tax. Whisky, for example, and other spirits, are cheaper in Rhodes than London and New York and so is petrol. Tourists benefit greatly from these concessions and other bargains are suiting materials, furs and jewellery. On the other hand items imported from Athens or via Athens are likely to cost more than in the capital as they bear transportation costs as well as the municipal tax. The high price of foreign cigarettes, particularly British and American, is aimed at protecting the large Greek tobacco industry and the local Rhodian industry.

The port is served by three working harbours whose functions are distinctive and strictly separated. The most northerly, Mandraki, is of little commercial importance and is reserved chiefly for yachts and caiques. The Commercial Harbour handles the main items of trade and is also the haven for inter-island and large cruise vessels. Acandia is the least active harbour though it has considerable development potential and recent improvements have included a jetty 800m long. A small-scale boat-building and boat-repairing industry is based in Acandia.

8   RURAL SETTLEMENT AND HANDICRAFTS

SIXTY per cent of the island's population is officially classified as rural and the principal type of settlement is the nucleated village with populations that range from 200 to over 2,000 inhabitants. The close-built village (*chora* or *chorio*) is usually the focal point of a distinct natural and economic area and various settlements often have their own specialised products and home industries. Dispersion of the rural population in scattered dwellings is not common, though where water and soil resources are more plentiful the community sometimes consists of one large village and a number of tributary hamlets (Fig 20a). Real settlement dissemination, however, is rare, except for isolated huts occupied during certain periods of the year.

Although they are not strictly coastal, most Rhodian villages are in low-lying areas and in relatively easy access of the sea. Among the exceptions are Embona (population 1,170), Aghios Issidoros (1,011), Apolona (840), Laerma (677) and Psinthos (560) which are situated at altitudes of between 275 and 435m in parts of the island where low-altitude plains are rare. Another generalisation (Fig 21) is the decline in village size from north to south throughout the island. Some of the largest rural communities—Trianda (3,150), Kremasti (2,100) and Paradis-sion (1,900)—occupy the agriculturally prosperous coastal plain to the south-west of Rhodes city, and Trianda, itself, is fast developing suburban status. Along the eastern coast the largest settlements are Koskinou (1,211), Kallithies (1,534), Aphandou (2,551), Archangelos (2,918) and Malona (1,510).

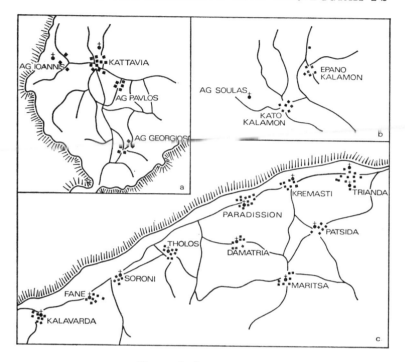

Fig 20 Settlement patterns

South of Aghios Issidoros villages rarely attain a size of 1,000 inhabitants and the largest communities of the extreme south are Apolakia (930), Kattavia (625) and Gennadion (705).

Throughout Rhodes, the tendency in the fields is the opposite of the tendency in the settlements they support: the more compact the nucleated village, the greater the degree of dispersal of holdings. The result is that villagers frequently have to travel long distances between their homes and fields and to circumvent this disadvantage a characteristic feature of the rural scene is a group of dwellings, known in Greece as *kalivia*, which are seasonally occupied, depending on the demands of the agricultural regime. Frequently, the *kalivia* develop into permanent settlements when a church and other facilities are added. Along

157

the coast small settlements act as ports for craft engaged in fishing or in local trade and transportation. They serve the needs of inland communities and are often called *skala* (landing-place), preceded by the name of the dependent settlement. Thus, Cameiros Skala formerly served the needs of the ancient settlement of Cameiros, a few kilometres away, and probably Kritinia. Today, the small port is used by fishermen from the off-shore island of Alimnia.

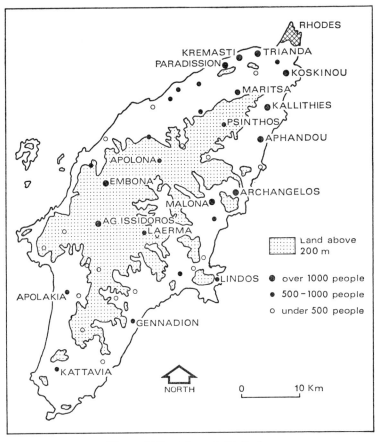

Fig 21   Village size and distribution

A similar type of settlement to the *kalivia*, but restricted to hilly districts, is the pair of villages prefixed by (*ep*)*ano* (upper) and *kato* (lower). Such settlements were formerly complimentary to each other and arose from transhumant and other seasonal agricultural activities. Usually they are located on the upper and lower slopes of valleys and illustrate the differences in agricultural practices at various altitudinal levels. An example of twin villages are Epano Kalamon and Kato Kalamon in the north-west of the island (Fig 20b).

VILLAGE SITING AND MORPHOLOGY

A great variety of factors are responsible for the choice of village sites and for the high degree of village nucleation that is common to Rhodes. Some primary criteria are the availability of water, agricultural convenience, and the natural gregariousness of the population. In the past security was also considered a significant factor and the compactness of Greek island villages has often been attributed to the needs of defence and the lack of money, so that the houses themselves formed a protective wall. Also for security reasons some settlements were built in hilly areas or in locations that were hidden from the sea. The large village of Aphandou, for example, occupies such a low situation that even from the road leading to the settlement only the rooftops are visible, whereas from the sea it is entirely hidden. Other villages such as Archangelos, Monolithos and Lindos stand in the shadows of medieval castles, but it appears that in the Byzantine period and certainly by the time of the Knights, the series of watchtowers and forts established around the entire circuit of the island provided adequate warning of danger from the sea and assured the protection of peasant families.

Individually fortified dwellings were also common in the past, but there are few remaining examples today. Trianda, however, has a *pirghos* house, or domestic fortress. It is a rectangular stone tower with a small round turret high in the north wall and the main windows are also set high. It was built at a time when protection against corsairs was a necessity. According to Currie the inhabitants of Trianda still refer to their houses as *pirghoi*, though they are often no higher or more defensive than a modern bungalow. An interesting collection of domestic fortresses is found at Lindos. These solidly built stone structures dating from the sixteenth century onwards, were once the dwellings of merchant-traders and sea captains.

Water supply, rather than defensive needs, has played a more decisive role in rural settlement and it is the key to both the distribution pattern of communities and to their degree of nucleation. Throughout the island, however, villages show a tendency to avoid river valleys, partly because most of the surface water-courses are temporary, and partly because such locations are liable to develop thermal inversions in winter and in summer to become unhealthily oppressive. An intermittent and unreliable water supply is not the answer to an agricultural community's water problems, and, consequently, settlements have been sited close to the only permanent sources of water, namely perennial springs or shallow aquifers where wells can be conveniently dug. The availability of water in areas of porous rocks has the effect of concentrating human settlement at fixed points and there is a marked contrast in the number and disposition of villages between areas of permeable and impermeable sub-soils. In the north-west, for example (Fig 20c), where the problem of water supply is less acute, the villages are evenly spaced, but they occupy sites that are both free from flooding and marginal to cultivation.

The convenience of land exploitation is another important factor in settlement location, although this often conflicts with the gregarious attitude of the Greeks and their liking for community life. The shortage of farmland has already been discussed and, until recently, under conditions of subsistent economy, the most desirable site for a village was one which permitted the greatest variety of agricultural possibilities.

Village limits tended to incorporate the widest range of soil types and terrain, thereby providing the community with areas of arable, pasture, rough-grazing and woodland. Today, with the fragmentation of holdings, the village is often badly placed to achieve agricultural efficiency, though closer contact between farm and farmland is now made feasible with technological advances. Natural sociability and the intense dislike of aloofness and private existence have been strong motives for the Rhodian farmer to maintain his homestead, if possible, within the community, thereby sacrificing efficiency and greater productivity for the advantages of close contact with other members of the village. Hutchinson's observations of Crete that 'the social Greek prefers to live in a crowded village among his friends and his café, even though he may have to walk miles to till his fields or trim his vines' apply equally to Rhodes.

The high degree of adaptation of villages to site factors makes it difficult to talk of a universal village morphology, although a few generalisations can be made. In low-lying areas there is a tendency to build on a grid-plan, whereas hillside villages are often sprawling in character and take their form from the contours of the site. Embona and Lindos are examples of the latter where the streets are narrow and irregular, often rising with stone steps from one terrace of houses to another. Improvements in communications this century have considerably altered the layout of many villages by introducing new focal points in relationship to main roads. The village of Gennadion, for example, straggles as far as the main east-coast road but the greater part of the settlement is off the road. Most of the modern village of Trianda also lies off the main road but a ribbon development of houses, cafés and garages, and, more recently, hotels, wends along the highway to Rhodes city.

All sizeable villages have a small, central square (*agora* or *platea*), which acts as the focal point of the community. Some are on a more grand scale than others and the large colonnaded square in a village the size of Eleoussa (300 inhabitants) stems from the fact that it housed the governor's palace during the Italian occupation. Around the central square are located cafés, shops, one or more churches, and, depending on the size of the village, a school and a public hall, the latter maintained like a club for social occasions. Some of the larger settlements have an administrative building, the *demarcheion*, but in the majority of villages the *demarchos* or mayor is to be found at his own place of business or residence.

HOUSE TYPES

The harmony between building and environment is shown more clearly in the traditional Rhodian house. The responsibility for house construction has always lain with the peasant farmer, who with limited resources was faced with the problem of providing a unit for both family and agricultural needs. The island remains faithful to the traditional design of a cubic house with a flat roof. Two types of roof have persisted in Greece from ancient times—a pitched roof which is confined largely to the mainland and the flat variety which is typical of the Aegean islands. Climate has been widely accepted as determining their distribution, the salient factors being the general problem of heat exclusion and variations in annual rainfall totals.

Cubic architecture is not peculiar to Rhodes, but is common throughout the Aegean and many parts of the Mediterranean. The Rhodian house, however, both externally and internally, is a variant of the Aegean type, in its distinctive and unmistakeable style. In its simplest form it consists of a single-room dwelling, built of local free-stone which is then whitewashed. The flat roof provides a terrace and generally it is supported by a structural arch which traverses the whole width of the house. In some villages the arch is replaced by a central pillar which supports a long wooden beam or two shorter ones. The pillar-

and-beam method is common in Embona (Fig 22c), but the problem in this type of construction is the scarcity of timber of sufficient length and strength for the necessary support. The arch method is more widespread as stone is plentiful and it has the advantage of being strong enough to support a second storey should that become necessary.

The roof terrace is about 25–30cm in thickness and is composed of several layers of reeds, osiers or dried seaweed, over which a layer of earth and gravel is placed. The whole is then finished with a layer of mud or mortar. When duly rolled the roof effectively keeps out winter rain, but tends to crack during the dry season and it is usual to add a fresh layer of earth at the end of every summer. The layered structure of the roof also intercepts the fiercer rays of the sun, keeping the interior of the house cool during the day, but re-radiating heat at night when temperatures can sometimes be uncomfortably low. Heat build-up during the day is also avoided by reducing the size and number of the windows, which are usually shuttered, and placing them high up to reduce ground radiation. The house is painted white, or some other light colour, to reflect a maximum of radiant heat. The traditional Rhodian house has the advantage of being easy and inexpensive to build, and, furthermore, the roof provides a suitably cool sleeping area during the summer months.

The interior takes its form from the structural arch or pillar which subdivides the living area into two sections of roughly equal size. The outer section is used for cooking and other domestic purposes and the inner part acts as a reception room and sleeping area. Traditionally, the latter is confined to one end of the inner room on a kind of dais which is bordered by a balustrade. This platform, known as the *sophas*, is the family bed and at one end the *krevatos*, or nuptial bed, would formerly have been covered by the *speveri*, an embroidered, tent-like curtain suspended from the ceiling and fanning out to cover the end of the platform. These bed-tents not only provided

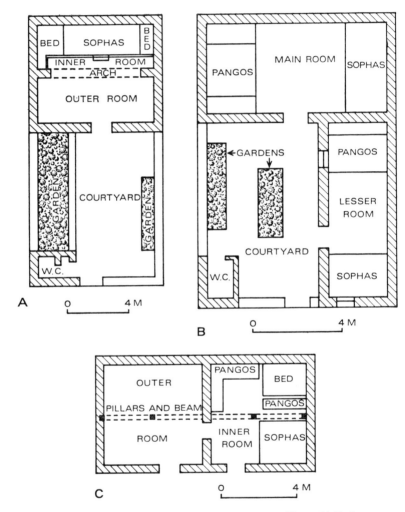

Fig 22 Traditional house plans: (a) Lindos; (b) Koskinou; (c) Embona

privacy but also preceded mosquito-curtains. A long wooden chest, the *pangos*, is placed alongside the marriage bed and another raised and balustraded area, the *ambataros*, is used for storing clothes and bedding. Throughout the island, this traditional arrangement is being modified considerably. The old beds are being replaced by European bedsteads and primitive forms of lighting such as candles and olive-oil lamps by paraffin lamps, and these by electricity. Many interiors still have very little furniture and usually the only fire-place is confined to the kitchen. A tradition that dies hard is the decorated wall in the reception area. This carries an impressive array of plates, pictures and embroidered napkins which usually form part of the bride's dowry. Most Rhodian houses also have their own domestic shrines where a candle burns continuously before the icon of the patron saint.

The single-room dwelling is the simplest form of Rhodian domestic architecture. More complicated house plans have developed with the addition of other rooms when the family increased or when sons brought their wives to their father's house. Two-storey flat-roofed houses are common on Rhodes and consist of a ground-level room with either an upper floor or a cellar. Equally general, however, are a series of low-level rooms, each with their own roofs, which communicate via a courtyard (Fig 22a and b). These designs are particularly common in Lindos and Koskinou where the plan is usually L-shape with the rooms enclosing the courtyard on two sides and thus preserving many elements of the ancient Greek house. The courtyard, which has direct access to the street, is generally rectangular and is itself an outdoor living area, particularly in summer. It provides complete privacy and one side, usually the wall of the adjacent house, provides a small vegetable and floral garden. When shaded and provided with greenery and water, the courtyard acts as a cooling well, lowering the ground temperature.

J. Hope has studied the various stages in the development of the Lindian courtyard houses. The oldest examples, dating from the sixteenth century, are built in styles derived from the Gothic of the Knights with Byzantine and oriental decoration. In their simplest form they consist of one large room of the type and arrangement already discussed, but located off a courtyard which communicates with the street by an ornamental gate (Fig 22a). The ceilings are elaborately painted and the beams rest on sculptured cornices. In a number of the early houses a stone staircase leads to an upper level from where, it is said, Lindian merchants could watch the arrival and departure of shipping. This tower room or 'captain's' room often spans the street and is supported by an arch which is structurally a continuation of the main support of the low-level room. During the nineteenth century small rooms were added to the existing main room, thus enclosing the courtyard on two sides. The main room was slept in by the head of the household, but during the day it was used only on special occasions. Many of the old houses of Lindos were destroyed in the earthquake of 1926 and were rebuilt on entirely new lines with extra rooms with roof terraces above them.

The individualism of the Rhodian is apparent in the exterior decoration of houses and street walls. A characteristic floor finish of rooms, courtyards, and in some cases, alleyways, is a pebble pavement set in clay or cement. The technique, known as *chocklaki*, is common to many places in Greece and the Mediterranean and the tradition on Rhodes can be traced back to at least the early Middle Ages. Coloured sea pebbles are often used, but in Lindos only black and white pebbles make up the intricate mosaics whose common designs include stars, circles, tridents, formalised flowers and cypresses. These floors are practical as well as decorative for when washed they retain their coolness. Other examples of functional decoration include ornamental devices for shedding rainwater from roofs, elegant chimneypots and, in the case of Lindos, ornate corbell details for the splayed corners of streets which enable pack-animals to negotiate junctions. The enrichment of façades also includes string courses, door and window mouldings and low-relief carvings of crosses and birds and roundels over main doors.

Since most Rhodian settlements have suffered from earthquakes, various structural devices have been incorporated into village and individual house designs. The staggering of back-to-back terraces according to the site factors is one anti-seismic method. Another construction is the arched buttress across streets which is most characteristic in Lindos and the old town of Rhodes.

In common with many parts of Greece, especially those areas which reap benefits from tourism, rural life on Rhodes is rapidly changing. This is reflected in modern house types which are gradually replacing, especially in the north, the traditional designs. The Agricultural Bank of Greece now provides credit for new construction and house improvement, and standardised building materials and approved house designs have been introduced. The newer houses are small one-storey dwellings built of hollow fired bricks. They can be speedily erected and their rapid spread is related to continued improvement in communications reinforced by better ideas and methods of hygiene. Change of materials, however, does not necessarily change the form of the house and a combination of home and economic unit is still prevalent. The major contrasts stem from the tiled pitched roofs of newer houses and their brightly painted exteriors.

LINDOS

The village of Lindos merits special discussion for a number of reasons: it is a settlement rich in history, it is a major tourist centre and, not least, it has been described as one of the most picturesque places in Greece. Its appearance and morphology, in the words of Lawrence Durrell, is 'of a scrupulous Aegean order, and perfect in its kind'. When the Italians built the east-coast road, they terminated the section leading to Lindos in a square on the outskirts of the village. This is still as far as motorised traffic can go and the lane-like streets of the settlement are suitable only for panniered mules and donkeys for which they were originally designed.

Modern Lindos has less than a thousand inhabitants, but in antiquity, prior to the establishment of the city of Rhodes, it was the leading maritime centre of the island with a population of around 16,000. Its power and commercial strength was not easily relinquished to Rhodes and Lindos continued as a trading centre throughout the medieval period. Under the Knights of St John the ancient acropolis was turned into a medieval fortress to protect the southern seas from Moslem forces. It still survives and surrounds the ruins of the Doric temple and the Byzantine church of Aghios Ioannis. Other early churches in the village, now being studied by archaeologists, include Aghios Georgios and Aghios Demetrius. The Hospitallers also built the Church of Our Lady of Lindos which is a fine example of Byzantine-influenced architecture.

With the departure of the Knights Lindos maintained its commercial importance, and influential merchants and shipowners developed trading connections with Turkey, Greece and the Middle East. This prosperous period is reflected in forty or so dwellings which date from the sixteenth century onwards. Many are now either closed or exist as museums with rich displays of Lindos plates, embroideries and domestic architecture. During the nineteenth century active trade came to an abrupt end and the settlement since this time has been left virtually untouched, except for the excavation and restoration work carried out by the Greeks and Italians, and for the damage caused by earthquakes.

Lindos, unlike Rhodes, developed naturally and its street plan is at first sight fairly chaotic (Fig 23). Its appearance is of irregularly clustered, flat-roofed buildings stretching round the acropolis towards the sea on both sides. The streets follow the

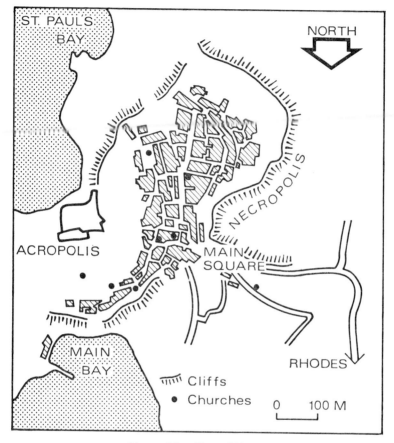

Fig 23   The village of Lindos

natural contours of the ground and the surrounding steep land
and cliff lines provide natural limits to the settlement, imposing
a compactness which contrasts strongly with the barrenness
of the hills adjoining it. Hope stresses the descending order of
visual scale that characterises the village—the massive form of
the acropolis, the smaller units of the village itself and, finally,
the still smaller units of chapels and houses outside the main
settlement. He attributes the visual success of Lindos to this

image of decreasing scale, to the compactness of the village and to the recurrence of a few basic building patterns and units. The repetition of design is best illustrated in the courtyard house for although no two are identical they all follow the same general plan. Throughout the village each house unit has been added to another to form blocks of up to twenty houses around which the streets and lanes have been fitted.

The streets of the village vary in width from the 1·5m minimum, determined by the size of a loaded donkey or mule, to about 2·5 to 3m in the main thoroughfares. With the exception of the access area on the periphery, Lindos has no public spaces or squares, and communal buildings such as shops, cafés and churches are scattered throughout the village, but usually they are located at the crossings of the most frequented routes. From the motorised square the village plan resolves itself into three principal streets which lead from it, one serving the western part of the settlement, another leading to the school, main harbour and acropolis, and a central one which serves as the main axis of village life.

Modern Lindos is a poor village and has suffered greatly from depopulation. Its water supply is still inadequate and much of it comes from an underground cistern built during antiquity. The electricity supply is also limited and is often switched on only for a few hours each night. Earthquakes have caused great destruction and the southern end, towards the Port of St Paul, has been the most severely damaged and is now mostly in ruins. Most of the historic buildings date from after the great earthquake of 1481 which completed the devastation wrought by the unsuccessful Turkish siege of 1480. An equally disastrous earthquake occurred in 1926.

Tourism is now a major industry in Lindos but many authorities view it with suspicion and fear that unplanned development will be a major threat to the village. Lindos is under the protection of the Greek Archaeological Society which succeeded the Italian Department of Antiquities. Its primary concern is the preservation of the village and its development along visually appropriate lines. Such a policy is of major importance in combating the increasingly powerful development pressures of a tourist village.

In the past Rhodian villages developed their own specialised products and home industries. The impact of tourism is particularly felt in the revival of these traditional handicrafts which today must be seen functioning solely in response to demands created by the souvenir and gift market. In 1966 the Greek government, through the Committee for Workshop Credit, approved the conditions whereby loans are granted to small production units. The aim is to promote the handicraft branch of manufacturing activity, increase productivity and develop new markets at home and abroad. Rhodes city, itself, is a significant market for handicraft products, but locally produced items also fill the tourist and souvenir shops in Athens and other centres throughout Greece. Handwoven goods, embroideries, ceramics, light furniture, leather and metal goods are the main Rhodian specialisations and the prefecture administration is making every effort to promote handicraft activity which now contributes decisively to the island's income and balance of payments. The Panhellenic Exhibition of Handicrafts is held at Kremasti.

Rhodes has always been a centre for ceramic production and the various decorative patterns that adorn contemporary vases and plates are derived from early times. During the centuries BC the designs were influenced by the metal-working and carpet-making traditions of the East which explains why the style became known as 'orientalistic'. Illustrations on plates and vases depict animals and birds, with supplementary decorative motifs of plant life. They also include symmetrical compositions made up of horizontal bands which together with the ornamental devices used to fill in empty spaces are reminiscent of Assyrian sculpture and textile designs of the Orient.

Throughout the classical period Rhodian pottery was influenced by the Attic style and the decoration was often a pictorial achievement of a very high standard. There are a few surviving examples of ceramic art belonging to the Hellenistic age, notably a number of long-neck jugs, but in the centuries that followed pottery ceased to be a craft of distinction and refinement. Instead, workshops concentrated on the production of cheaper earthenware items for everyday use, although their styles followed closely classical and earlier forms.

The revival of the industry in the Middle Ages is attributed to the Knights of St John. There is a story, unconfirmed, that in the fourteenth century the Knights captured a Levantine ship in which some Persian and Damascene potters were travelling. They were brought to Lindos where they were forced to work using local clay and a sand that was suitable for glazing. The considerable output of Lindian plates and vases found ready markets throughout Europe and the products were decorated with designs of Persian inspiration, including stylised flowers, animals and ships. Under the Turks the industry was transferred to Rhodes city and wide markets for Rhodian ceramics existed in Europe and Turkey.

Examples of the famous 'Lindos' ware are now the treasures of European museums but the designs and colours provide the inspiration for the contemporary industry. This was first organised on a systematic basis with the foundation of the 'Icarus' pottery in 1928. The modern industry has altered its aims from the production of purely decorative items to a combination of the decorative and functional. The chief production centres are Rhodes, Trianda, Paradission and Archangelos.

The art of embroidery also stretches back to ancient times. It is still common for girls to be taught embroidery and weaving from an early age, preparing articles which will later form part of their dowry. The current style seems to have been derived

172

from late Byzantine work and many of the traditional designs are reminiscent of ecclesiastical symbolism—peacocks, the tree of life, birds and the cross. It is significant that Byzantine words connected with embroidery and weaving abound and many of them remain in current use. For example, there are woven embroideries or tapestries made on the *voua* (loom) by *lefantaries* (women weavers), and other anachronistic terms are common.

Many of the traditional designs can be seen on the various local costumes of Rhodes, though sadly, these are either confined to museums or appear only during festivals. Another rare item is the famous *speveri*, the highly decorative tent-like canopy which covered the bridal bed. Embroidered sheets also took priority in decorating the house.

The principal centre for embroidery since Byzantine times has been Lindos. Like pottery, the industry has been placed on a commercial footing and it is common for dealers to employ skilled women who work on articles at home. Typical products are napkins, table-cloths and runners and embroidered pictures. Crochet and lace-work is also practised.

Byzantium has been the main source of inspiration for goldsmiths and silversmiths too, many of whom settled in Rhodes from Constantinople, Smyrna and Mersin. This century, however, styles in jewellery were influenced by Italian craftsmen who leaned more towards medieval designs. Woodcarving illustrates both Byzantine and Frankish influence, though the craft survives only on a limited scale today and there is little modern work that can compare with the carved altar screens at churches in Lindos, Gennadion, Trianda and other villages. A recent development has been the carving of olive-wood which is useful for both ornaments and utensils. Only a few craftsmen survive to produce larger items of furniture.

Two relatively new crafts are carpet-making and the manufacture of wrought-iron products. The former was introduced from Asia Minor following the Turkish–Greek exchanges of population in the 1920s. The refugees developed the 'Rhodian' carpet which incorporated both eastern and local designs. After 1936 the industry was encouraged by the Italians through subsidies and expert supervision and the models were the 'Turkish' carpets of Ushak, Isbarta and Bokhara. The industry remains small and like embroidered products, carpets are woven by skilled craftswomen under a retainer. Aphandou is an important production centre.

The wrought-iron industry emerged to meet the decorative requirements of the period around 1930 when Italian public buildings were being erected in Rhodes city. Initially its development was the work of the Italian craftsman, Carlo Roselli, who was christened 'magno de ferro batuto' (the wizard of wrought iron). Ornamental gates, balconies, chandeliers and lamps were the typical products and the influence of medieval Rhodes was apparent in their style and design. Several workshops now exist producing articles of both functional and decorative value for the Greek and tourist markets.

9   A COMPENDIUM FOR VISITORS

THIS chapter fills in some details of Rhodian life omitted from the earlier pages, but, primarily, it is meant to help the visitor in the island. The earlier chapters were neither designed nor intended as a tourist guide to Rhodes. Their object was to introduce the complexities of the island and its people through an analysis of geography, history and contemporary life. Information expected from a standard guidebook may be culled from the previous pages, though no attempt was made to provide detailed tourist itineraries or descriptions of panoramic views. Such an approach would have destroyed the object of this book. What Rhodes has to offer in scenery and historical remains is a matter of the traveller's own choice, interests and tastes.

The following pages provide a series of miscellaneous topics which will prove useful to those people whose interest in Rhodes has been aroused and who contemplate a visit to the island. Further information of high quality and accuracy may be obtained from the offices of the National Tourist Organisation of Greece in most major cities in the world and some useful tourist guides are listed in the bibliography. Strongly recommended for its accuracy of detail is Jean Currie's *The Travellers' Guide to Rhodes and the Dodecanese* (1970).

DOCUMENTS AND FORMALITIES

To enter Rhodes directly, or via other Greek centres, citizens of the United Kingdom and the United States require valid passports which entitle them to stay for periods up to three months, for British subjects, and up to two months for United States subjects without prior Greek consular visas. For extended periods visitors are required to present themselves twenty days before the expiry date, either at the Aliens Department, Athens, or at the police authority of the district, where application for an extension can be made.

Greece has certain currency regulations concerning the amount of drachmae in bank notes which persons, Greek or foreign, may bring in or take out of the country. Usually this is limited to 750 (£10, $25 in 1973) and all currency should be declared at customs control points on entering Greece. Customs exemptions on articles and goods are much the same as for Britain and the United States provided they are personal effects. Gifts for a third party are also exempt of duty provided their combined value does not exceed the equivalent of $150 (£60) and on condition that they are not being imported for sale. It should be remembered that owing to tax concessions current throughout the Dodecanese, Rhodes has its own customs and luggage may be examined on leaving the island or on entering another part of Greece.

THE CITY OF RHODES

Whether arriving by sea or by air the visitor to the island will inevitably disembark in Rhodes city. As the only urban centre on the island it functions as the commercial and administrative capital and earns for itself the title 'Metropolis', by which it is known to native Rhodians. The city's present population of 28,000 inhabitants is equivalent to 40 per cent of the island's total, but during the months of June, July and August this figure is almost doubled by the influx of tourists.

The various stages in the development of the island's capital have been discussed in earlier chapters, and today the city is a living monument to the island's long and chequered history.

Each phase of history is recalled in the monuments it has bequeathed and the often strange rapprochement of different architectural styles gives the city its original and distinctive air. By Greek standards, Rhodes has more pride in appearance and more urban order and cleanliness than is common for most provincial towns.

The main morphological and visual contrasts are between the old town with its amalgam of medieval and Turkish styles and the new town built outside the fortress and enclosing it on all sides except the seaward. The old quarter (Fig 24) has not altered substantially from that of the Turkish period and sections of it, particularly in the south-east, suffer from the needs of physical renewal. Its morphology remains one of tortuous streets and back alleyways, prohibiting motorised traffic in much of the area and making orientation confusing in the extreme. The plan resolves itself in a number of principal streets of which Socrates Street, and its continuation as Aristotelos and Pindarou Streets, forms the main commercial artery. Other major thoroughfares include Hippodamus, Fanourios, Pythago-

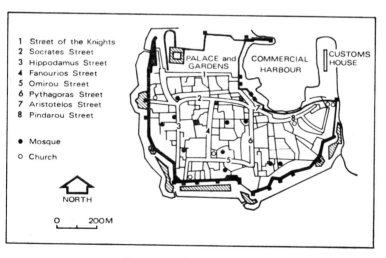

1 Street of the Knights
2 Socrates Street
3 Hippodamus Street
4 Fanourios Street
5 Omirou Street
6 Pythagoras Street
7 Aristotelos Street
8 Pindarou Street

● Mosque
○ Church

NORTH

0   200M

Fig 24   Rhodes, the old town

ras and Omirou Streets. Socrates Street extends from the Mosque of Suleiman to Hippocrates Square and is very much alive with the everyday activities of the local population. Its numerous shops, workrooms, cafés and taverns, however, are largely dependent on the tourist traffic. This street, together with many others in the old town, has the feel of the Orient with its corbelled balconies, projecting upper storeys and dark alleyways leading off to vaulted houses. Exploration of the old town is an exercise in discovery and the rewards are visual surprises on almost every turning.

In contrast, the modern extension of Rhodes is built on a more spacious and regular plan (Fig 25). Initially, it dates from the Turkish period when the Greeks working within the old town were not permitted to remain within the walls at night. Its rapid development since 1912 has united the various Greek suburbs which governed the street plan of later extensions. The commercial quarter of the new town lies to the north of the fortress and extends to Kumburnu Point. It includes the old Greek suburbs of Masari and Neochori but much of its fabric is modern.

Under the Italian regime a new commercial quarter was developed along the shores of Mandraki Harbour and the public buildings lining the waterfront were designed in various monumental styles. The major buildings include the Town Hall, the Post Office and the National Theatre, all built in a Mussolinian square style, characteristic of the Fascist genre. In contrast is the former Governor's Palace, now the Nomarchia or Prefecture, which is built in a Venetian-Gothic style with marble decoration and an arcaded façade. Dominating the harbour entrance is the Cathedral or Church of the Evangelist, built in 1925 on the model of the Church of St John in the old town which was destroyed in 1856. Fronting Mandraki, the Italians also built a large polygonal market in a Turkish style and this, together with the cafés and restaurants that surround it, acts today as the focal point and social centre of the new town.

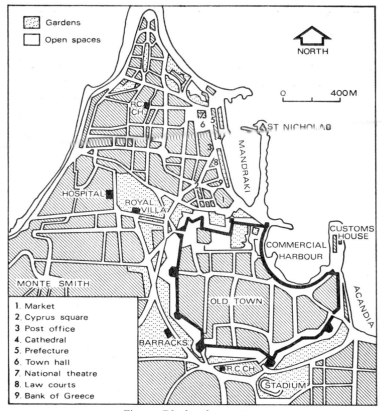

Fig 25 Rhodes, the new town

The modern business section lies behind the market in a series of streets leading off from Cyprus Square.

The northern section of the new town also contains the majority of hotels and tourist organisations. The area around and to the north of Constantine Avenue is almost exclusively devoted to the tourist industry. The exception is King Paul Square which contains the Agricultural Bank, the Welfare Centre, the Migration Department and other national institutions.

The southern and western districts of the new town contrast

strongly with the administrative and commercial functions of the northern section. The south has the densest population and contains most of the city's modest industries. It corresponds to the old Greek neighbourhoods of St Anargyrous, St Anastasia, St Nicholas and St George. Westwards, development extends to the slopes of Monte Smith and spreads freely over the landscape in a succession of larger houses and villas, situated amongst greenery and gardens. The harmonious composition gives the impression of an extensive ring of suburbs rather than a strict adjunct to the urban area.

HEALTH AND MEDICINE

The International Sanitary Regulations apply in Greece in addition to those laid down by the 1959 Council of Europe and by local law. Rarely are vaccination certificates required of travellers from Western Europe and North America, though smallpox and cholera scares sometimes necessitate proof of immunity. The local population is safeguarded against sickness and disability by a number of national insurance schemes and the visitor is advised to take out a policy covering himself against illness as medical treatment can be expensive.

The city of Rhodes is well supplied with doctors and specialists and in the majority of villages doctors are on hand or on call. The city has its main hospital with full medical facilities and there is also an Institute of Common Health. Dentists and opticians are available and numerous chemists sell familiar medicines. The chemists are often extremely thorough, though by no means infallible, in diagnosing minor complaints like stomach upsets and heatstroke.

In the city good and safe drinking-water is available and the majority of villages have chemically treated supplies. Bottled mineral water is available when in doubt. The presence of a pitcher of water in village rooms means that the tap water is *not* safe to drink.

A COMPENDIUM FOR VISITORS

CURRENCY AND BANKING

The drachma is the exclusive legal tender on Rhodes though foreign currency and travellers' cheques are readily exchangeable. The drachma is divided into 100 lepta and coinage is in denominations of 5, 10, 20 and 50 lepta, and 1, 2, 5, 10 and 20 drachmae. Bank notes are in denominations of 50, 100, 500 and 1,000 drachmae. In January 1973, 100 drachmae were equivalent to £1.25 and US $3.23.

The major banks of Greece, including the National Bank of Greece, the Ionian and Popular Bank and the Commercial Bank of Greece have offices in the city and branches in some of the larger villages. To assist the visitor, some banks have foreign exchange offices and travellers' cheques can be cashed in many hotels, restaurants and shops.

TELEPHONE AND POSTAL SERVICES

The Telecommunication Organisation of Greece (OTE) is housed in the same building as the Post Office in Mandraki. Rhodes has an automatic exchange and direct calls can be made to over a hundred centres in Greece as well as to the villages of Trianda and Kremasti on the island. Other calls are made through the normal trunk-line exchange and, via Athens, it is possible to telephone the United States, Canada, Britain and the majority of Western European countries. Telephones are available at most pavement kiosks and a few public call-boxes are located around the town. There is at least one telephone available in all rural settlements.

The Post Office is open seven days a week and surface and air mail rates for letters and packages vary for respective destinations.

LANGUAGE

The Greek language can often be something of a problem to the visitor, although Rhodes city is cosmopolitan during summer and English, French, Italian, German and Swedish are widely understood in hotels, tourist offices and in many shops and restaurants. It is in the country that the major difficulties in communications are encountered but even here almost every village, no matter how isolated, has its 'Greek-American', an ex-immigrant who has returned to live out his retirement in his native village. Generally his unpolished English is much better than the tourist's attempt at Greek.

Visitors to Rhodes, however, are strongly advised to be familiar at least with the Greek alphabet. This is indispensable in reading street and bus signs and once mastered the number of Greek words that have their direct equivalent in English will be appreciated. No one can pretend that Modern Greek, with its complex grammar and experimental and fluid form, is easy to learn, but any attempt on the part of the visitor to speak the local language is warmly appreciated by the Rhodians. For those who want to see the non-tourist side of the island a few Greek words and phrases often lead to invitations for coffee and ouzo, fishing trips and sometimes overnight accommodation in a villager's home.

ACCOMMODATION

The proliferation of hotel accommodation now means that Rhodes is the only Greek city, apart from Athens, that offers a wide selection of hotels ranging from the luxury category to comfortable pensions. A number of the higher-grade establishments have private beaches, swimming pools and sports facilities, and recently, the bungalow complex has increased in popularity. Away from the city, however, accommodation is limited and simple, though plans for modern hotels for other parts of the island are in preparation. In most villages rooms may be rented in private houses at modest payment and the local policeman or village president usually assists in finding suitable accommodation. It is also worth while remembering that most monasteries have guest quarters and there is no bar on women. Sometimes meals are provided and a monetary donation is in order on leaving.

Annually, the National Tourist Organisation supplies a list of new and established hotels with their categories and prices. Hotels are classified by the government and charges are set within strict limits. The charge appropriate to the room is entered in a notice, usually fixed to the inside of the door, and there are a number of reductions which operate in favour of the visitor, including off-season rates. Hotels are classified into AA or L (luxury), A, B, C, D and E categories and are assigned on the basis of such facilities as air conditioning, hot running water, telephones in rooms etc. These categories can be some-what misleading, however, for with the great spate of hotel construction many of the modern B and C establishments often offer better value in terms of amenities than an old A-class hotel.

Rhodes has three luxury hotels—Grand Summer Palace, Hotel des Roses and Miramare Beach Hotel and the former has been described as one of the best-equipped hotels in Europe. In addition the city and its surroundings has 18 A-class, 18 B-class, 53 C-class and over 40 D- and E-class establishments, though accommodation in the latter two categories can be spartan. There is a Youth Hostel in the city but this is not affili-ated to the YHA of Greece

During the height of summer it is advisable to reserve accom-modation well in advance as block bookings by tour operators considerably reduce the number of beds available in July, August and September. It is possible to rent a villa or house on Rhodes and information is obtainable from the NTO in the city.

No exaggerated claims can be made for Rhodian cuisine. It is limited in range and tends to be savoury rather than subtle. The standard of home cooking is often excellent, but rarely is this maintained in restaurants and *tavernas* where interest in quality, temperature and presentation is sadly lacking. In many large hotels, and in the main restaurants, the cuisine is 'international', in response to the cosmopolitan clientèle, and attempts to combine the 'delicacy' of continental cuisine with the 'succulence' of the Orient sometimes comes off.

The predominant influence on Rhodian cooking is Turkish and much of the island food is similar to that of Greece as a whole. The main ingredients are olive oil, tomatoes, onions, garlic and synthetic fats and there is a liberal use of herbs and sauces in all dishes. The ubiquitous Greek dishes, including *souvlakia* (pieces of veal, lamb or pork grilled on a skewer), *dolmades* (vine or cabbage leaves stuffed with meat and rice), *keftedes* (savoury meat balls) and *mousaka* (minced meat and aubergine pie) are equally common on Rhodes. Other common denominators are a wide range of soups, often eaten as a main course, and various spaghetti and macaroni dishes. Of the soups, the best known is *avgolemono*, a soup thickened with egg and flavoured with lemon.

Rhodes is not a big meat-eating island. Apart from a few areas of good grazing land, the rest of the island provides poor fodder for cattle and much of the meat supply has to be imported. The ingenious Greeks over the centuries have learned to make the best of what they have and eat what might otherwise be tough and flavourless meat finely minced with a rich anthology of flavouring.

The staple meat is some form of lamb-sheep-mutton which is prepared in an infinite variety of ways. In rural areas the traditional Greek oven cooking is done in a beehive-shaped structure situated at the side of the house or in the courtyard. Families who have no oven often send their own food to be cooked in the local bakery. Veal, beef and pork is obtainable in the capital but, in the country, lamb and chicken are the only common meat dishes.

Fish are more of a rarity than one would expect on an island and the majority of fish dishes are expensive. Rhodes city has a number of restaurants where fish is served and sold by the kilo and is sent to the table complete with the head, which is considered the best part by many Greeks. Most meals are eaten with a green salad (*horiatiki*) comprising tomatoes, peppers, onions, cucumbers and cheese. Much of the island's fruit and vegetable produce is widely available and of good quality, and individual vegetable dishes of beans, aubergines, marrows, spinach and potatoes also accompany a main dish. The availability of fruits varies according to the season and the most common are peaches, grapes, melons, water-melons, figs, citrus fruits and also apples, pears, pomegranates and apricots.

Like all Greeks the Rhodians have a very sweet tooth and *zacharoplasteia* (pastry shops) abound in the capital, and most villages have at least one. Typical Greco-Turkish sweets are *kataifi*, *baclava* and *galatoboureko*, made from *filo* (paper-thin pastry sheets) and filled with nuts, spices and syrups. *Rizogalo* (rice pudding containing egg and lemon) and *yiaourti* (yoghourt) with sugar or honey are equally popular. Rhodians, however, rarely end their meals with puddings and pies but content themselves with fresh fruit. The *zacharoplasteion* is more a place to linger and relax in during the siesta break or late into the evenings.

The Rhodians are dedicated to coffee-drinking which can be regarded as a national pastime. Coffee is served Turkish style and there are three main varieties—*gliko*, meaning sweet; *metrios*, which is made with half sugar and half coffee, and *sketos*, made without sugar. The instant varieties, known through-

M

out Greece as Nescafé, are readily available and some restaurants serve espresso coffee.

Rhodian wines go well with the local food and Lindos Blanc Sec and the red Chevalier de Rhodes are produced on the island. There are also resinated (retsina) and unresinated varieties of wine and a large range of dessert wines. As elsewhere in Greece ouzo is the spirit of the island. It is made by distilling the crushed mash after the wine-juice has been pressed from the grapes, with anisette added to give a slight flavour. Brandy is another popular aperitif and the famous brand, Metaxa, is available in three-, five- or seven-star quality. Both ouzo and brandy are served with a plate of *mezedes* consisting of small pieces of fried liver, sardines, olives, fish roe, egg, tomato, cheese, cucumber and so on. Beer is popular but, compared with ouzo and brandy, it is expensive. Alpha, Fix and Amstel brands are available as well as a number of bottled continental beers. The greatest delicacy, however, is a glass of cold water. This forms an integral part of every Greek meal and is also served with cakes, coffee, ice cream, etc.

ENTERTAINMENTS

As previously stated, the Rhodian has undemanding tastes when it comes to entertainment. The great attachment of the Greeks to life in general, their inexhaustible imagination and their aptitude for improvisation, has developed for the country as a whole a type of entertainment typical and peculiar to its people. Entertainment on Rhodes has been greatly influenced by the island's climate. Sunny days and clear, mild, summer nights prompt the Rhodian to leave the house and seek relaxation out of doors in natural surroundings. The nocturnal habit is an important national characteristic and open-air cafés, pastry shops and restaurants are often full right through to the early morning hours. Rhodes city has many establishments, large and small, which offer meals to the accompaniment of music, while plenty of popular night *bouzoukia* restaurants and bars also offer meals, wine and Greek songs. Discothèques are equally common during the summer tourist season and Rhodes has one of the three casinos in operation in Greece. It is located in the luxurious Grand Summer Palace Hotel and gambling includes roulette, baccarat, chemin de fer and Black Jack. Stakes are accepted from a minimum of 20 drachmae to a maximum of 20,000 drachmae. The city also has a municipal theatre, which among other things, puts on displays of Greek dances and there are a number of indoor and open-air cinemas. The popular sound and light presentation, organised by the NTO, is held within the gardens adjacent to the Palace of the Grand Master. The performance takes the audience back to the Middle Ages, the Crusades, Suleiman the Magnificent and the rise of the Ottoman Empire in the eastern Mediterranean.

THE PRESS

Like all Greeks, the Rhodians are voracious newspaper-readers. This provides them with the necessary ammunition for conversation and debate in cafés and coffee-houses. A few local papers, generally weeklies, are published on Rhodes, but the influential newsprint comes from Athens, arriving by plane on the morning of publication. The dailies are sold by newspaper vendors or are obtainable from pavement kiosks. From Rhodes city newspapers reach other parts of the island by bus, taxi, or private car, but it may take a few days before the current news reaches some of the more remote villages. In rural areas the newspaper is the prize possession of the coffee-house and it is eagerly passed from client to client. Foreign newspapers are also readily available in Rhodes city. These are air mail editions and generally arrive one or two days after publication. The availability of English, French, German, Italian and Scandinavian dailies reflect the tourist trade of the city. The foreign papers are avidly read by the Greeks as their own national dailies are still subject to censorship.

SPORTS

The Rhodians indulge in most of the sports common throughout Europe. Swimming is the most popular. For beaches with bathing installations a small entrance fee is charged, but excellent natural beaches are found at Faliraki, Lindos, Aphandou and throughout the island. Associated water sports include skin-diving, sailing, canoeing, water-skiing and fishing. No permit is needed for sea-fishing, but there are certain restrictions on the use of spears and fishing-guns. For the yachting enthusiast Mandraki Harbour provides all the necessary services and Lindos Bay provides a suitable anchorage. Tennis courts and a stadium for football and tournaments are located in Rhodes city.

The island still has a fair amount of small game and hunting is a fast-developing sport. Hare-hunting is conducted from Aphandou, and Trianda and Aphandou have organised partridge-shooting. Good shooting during the season is found in the cedar, pine and cypress woods of Prophitis Elias.

MUSEUMS AND MONUMENTS

Many visitors are attracted to Rhodes solely on account of its rich archaeological and historical remains. It is possible to obtain a complete view of the island's history from Rhodes city alone, but a wealth of archaeological sites and historic buildings is found throughout the island. Rhodes has its own archaeological service and inspector of antiquities whose duties include the administration and protection of the island's relics of the past. The Archaeological Museum, housed in the former Hospital of the Knights, contains collections of coins and pottery from the sites of Cameiros and Ialysos and also funerary steles

188

and works of the Rhodian sculptors. The restored and modern-
ised Palace of the Grand Master is open to the public and it
contains a number of ancient mosaics and statues from the island
of Kos. Conducted tours can also be made of the medieval walls
and battlements. The hours during which museums and
archaeological sites are open to the public vary with the season'
and entrance fees range according to the location and the extent
and importance of the ruins.

For the Byzantine enthusiast many of the churches and
chapels of the countryside are of considerable historical and
artistic interest. The keys are generally kept by the local priest
or an unofficial curator in the village.

The small folk museum in the old town of Rhodes has a
collection of traditional costumes, furniture and pottery.
Similar displays can be seen in some of the old houses in Lindos.
Rhodes city has a municipal art gallery with paintings by
modern Greek artists and at the northernmost point of the city
is the Hydrobiological Institute. This is unique in Greece and
has a collection of embalmed marine life as well as an aquarium.

CHRONOLOGY OF MAJOR EVENTS

2500–1150 BC	Carian, Phoenician, Minoan and Achaean settlement
11th C BC	Dorian settlement and colonisation
700 BC (approx)	The Dorian Hexapolis
480 BC	Rhodes becomes subject to Athens
408 BC	Foundation of the city of Rhodes
323 BC	Death of Alexander the Great
305 BC	Demetrius Poliocetes lays siege to Rhodes
302 BC	Work starts on the colossus
227 BC	Earthquake destroys colossus and city
197 BC	Rhodes joins Rome against Macedon
166 BC	Rome makes Delos a free port
42 BC	Cassius lays siege and plunders Rhodes
AD 51	St Paul visits Rhodes
70–9	Rhodes incorporated into Roman Empire
395	Subdivision of Roman Empire
653ff	Arabs and Saracens sack Rhodes
1082	Alexos Comnenos grants Venetians trading privileges
1097ff	Rhodian harbours used during Crusades
1242	Genoese take Rhodes from Leon Gavalas
1309	The Knights of St John take Rhodes
1444	Sultan of Egypt lays siege to Rhodes
1453	Fall of Constantinople and end of Byzantine Empire
1480	The second siege by Mohammed the Conqueror

1522	The siege of Suleiman the Magnificent
1523	The Knights leave Rhodes
1522–1912	The Turkish occupation of Rhodes
1912–43	The Italians occupy Rhodes
1943	The fall of Italy and the German occupation
1945	British forces occupy Rhodes
1917	Rhodes and the Dodecanese united with Greece

ARMS AND DATES OF THE GRAND MASTERS (1309–1522)

Fig 26   The arms and dates of the Grand Masters of Rhodes

PRINCIPAL FEASTS AND HOLIDAYS

1 January	Feast of St Basil (public holiday)
6 January	Epiphany (public holiday)
7 January	Feast of St John the Baptist
2 February	Feast of the Purification of the Virgin
February–March	Carnival (the three weeks before Lent)
25 March	Independence Day (public holiday)
Easter	The cycle includes Maundy Thursday, Good Friday and Easter Saturday, Sunday and Monday
23 April	St George's Day
1 May	May Day (sometimes a public holiday)
Whit Monday	Public holiday
6 June	Feast of the Holy Spirit (public holiday)
15 June	Feast of St Amos, Faliraki
17 June	Feast of St Marina at Paradission, Koskinou etc
24 June	Nativity of St John the Baptist
29 June	St Peter and St Paul Day
30 July	Festival of St Soulas at Soroni
6 August	Dance festivals throughout the month
15 August	Feast of the Virgin (public holiday)
23 August	Feast of the Holy Merciful at Kremasti and Trianda
29 August	Feast of the execution of St John
8 September	Name-day of the Virgin
14 September	Festival of the Cross at Kallithies etc
26 October	Feast of St Demetrius

APPENDIX C

28 October	Ochi Day (public holiday)
31 November	Feast of St Andrew
December	The month of St Nicholas
25 December	Christmas Day

BIBLIOGRAPHY

ADMIRALTY, Naval Intelligence Division. *The Dodecanese*. London, 1943

ATIYA, A. S. *Crusade, Commerce and Culture*. London, 1962

BELABRUI, Γ. *Rhodes of the Knights*. Oxford, 1908

BOOTH, C. D. *Italy's Aegean Possessions*. London, 1928

BRADFORD, E. *The Companion Guide to the Greek Islands*. London, 1963

BRADFORD, J. 'Aerial Discoveries in Rhodes', *Antiquaries Journal*, 36, 57–69 (1956)

BROCKMAN, E. *The Two Sieges of Rhodes*. London, 1969

CASAVIS, J. N. *Italian Atrocities in Grecian Dodecanese*. Dodecanese League of America, 1936

——. *The Region of the Dodecanese and Its Persecution by Italy*. Dodecanese League of America, 1937

CHURCHILL, W. S. *The Second World War*, vol 5. London, 1952

CURRIE, J. *The Travellers' Guide to Rhodes and the Dodecanese*. London, 1970

DAMASKENIDES, A. N. 'Problems of the Greek Rural Economy', *Balkan Studies*, vol 6, no 1, 1965

DERYENN, G. *Rhodes and the Dodecanese* (in French). Paris, 1962

DURRELL, L. *Reflections on a Marine Venus*. London, 1969

FRIEDL, E. *Vasilika, A Village in Modern Greece*. New York, 1962

GABRIEL, A. *The City of Rhodes* (in French). Paris, 1921

GUTLAND, E. A. *International History of City Development*, vol 4: *Urban Development in Southern Europe: Italy and Greece*. London, 1969

HADJIMIKHALI, A. *Greek Folk Art* (in Greek). Athens, 1925

HALE, J. R. (ed). *Europe in the Late Middle Ages*. London, 1965

HARTOFILI, N. J. *Rhodes* (English translation). Athens, 1967

HEURTLEY, W. A. (et al). *A Short History of Greece*. Cambridge, 1965

HOPE, J. 'Lindos, Isle of Rhodes', *Ekistics*, 23 (1967)

HUTCHINSON, R. W. *Prehistoric Crete*. London, 1965

KASPERSON, R. E. *The Dodecanese: Diversity and Unity in Island Politics*. Department of Geography, Research Paper no 108, Chicago, 1966

KONDIS, I. D. *Contribution to the Study of the Street Plan of Rhodes*. Rhodes, 1954

LOJACONO, P. 'The Palace of the Grand Master of Rhodes' (in Italian), *Clara Rhodos*, I (1928)

BIBLIOGRAPHY

MATTON, R. *Rhodes* (in French). Collection of the French Institute. Athens, 1966

MCEVEDY, C. *Atlas of Ancient History.* London, 1967

——. *Atlas of Medieval History.* London, 1961

MACKENDRICK, P. *The Greek Stones Speak.* London, 1962

MAJURI, A. and JACOPI, G. 'Monuments of Crusader Art', *Clara Rhodos*, I (1928)

MARINATOS, S. 'The Volcanic Destruction of Minoan Crete', *Antiquity*, 6 (1939)

MEGAS, G. A. *The Folk House of the Dodecanese* (in Greek). Athens, 1949

——. *The Greek House: Its Evolution and Its Relation to the Houses of Other Balkan Peoples* (in Greek). Athens, 1949

MULLER-WIENER, W. *Castles of the Crusaders.* London, 1966

NEWTON, C. *Travels and Discoveries in the Levant.* London, 1865

O'NEIL, B. H. St J. 'Rhodes and the Origin of the Bastion', *Antiquaries Journal*, 34, 44–54 (1954)

SANDERS, I. T. *Rainbow in the Rock—The People of Rural Greece.* Cambridge, 1962

SMITH, D. E. (et al). 'A Study of the Architecture of Lindos', *Ekistics*, 22 (1966)

TARN, W. *Hellenistic Civilisation.* London, 1959

TARSOULA, A. *The Dodecanese* (in Greek). Athens, 1947

THAKERAY, W. M. *Notes of a Journey from Cornhill to Grand Cairo.* London, 1886

THOMPSON, K. *Farm Fragmentation in Greece.* Athens, 1963

TORR, C. *Rhodes in Ancient Times.* Cambridge, 1885

——. *Rhodes in Modern Times.* Cambridge, 1887

——. *Rhodes under the Byzantines.* Cambridge, 1886

TOY, S. *A History of Fortifications.* London, 1955

VASILIEV, A. A. *History of the Byzantine Empire.* Madison & Milwaukee, 1964

VOLONAKIS, M. *The Island of Roses and Her Eleven Sisters.* London, 1922

——. *National Claims of the Dodecanese.* London, 1922

VOURAS, P. P. 'The Development of the Resources of the Island of Rhodes under Turkish Rule, 1522–1911', *Balkan Studies*, vol 4, no 1 (1963)

WACE, A. J. B. *Mediterranean and Near Eastern Embroideries.* London, 1935

ZERVOS, S. G. *Rhodes* (in French). Paris, 1921

ACKNOWLEDGEMENTS

AMONG the many individuals and organisations who helped me in collecting material contained in this book I wish, particularly, to thank the staff of the Information Department of the Greek Embassy, London, and the staffs of the National Tourist Organisation of Greece in Rhodes, Athens and London. I am also indebted to the many authors, ancient and modern, who have published on Rhodes and covered many aspects of the field before me.

On the practical side I wish to extend my sincere thanks for the help and co-operation received from the secretarial and technical staffs of the Department of Geography, University of Strathclyde, Glasgow. The maps and diagrams were expertly drawn by Miss D. C. Evans and Miss L. M. Gilchrist of the cartographic unit and the majority of the photographs were processed by Mr B. J. Reeves of the photographic unit. In this connection I would also like to thank Mr I. Barclay for his help with the photographic material and Mr A. Erskine for his advice on architectural terms. My gratitude also goes to Miss A. Laing who organised the typing schedule and to Mrs J. C. Simpson for her careful typing of the manuscript and valid criticism of my spelling and punctuation.

Acknowledgements are due to Jonathan Cape Ltd and Bobbs-Merrill Company Inc for permission to include the coats of arms of the Grand Masters of the Order of St John from *The Travellers' Guide to Rhodes and the Dodecanese* by Jean Currie.

Finally, I would like to express my thanks to Mr M. M. Johnstone for the skill with which he edited, and greatly improved, some of my original chapters.

INDEX

198

INDEX